John Henry Moss

BASEBALL'S MIRACLE MAN

John Henry Moss

BASEBALL'S MIRACLE MAN

BOB TERRELL

RIDGETOP BOOKS
Fairview, North Carolina

Grateful appreciation goes to Bill Ballew, director of media relations with the Asheville Tourists, for his careful reading of this manuscript. Ballew is the author of several baseball-related books and with Bob Terrell wrote Bob's autobiography, *BOB—My Father Was 'Mr. Terrell.'*

The South Atlantic League Media Guide and Record Book provided data for many of the facts and stats of the Appendix.

All photographs are from the John Henry Moss Collection. The photograph appearing on page 54 is by Bill Setliff Photography, and the photograph on page 107 is by DeMaine Photography.

© 2008 Bob Terrell

Ridgetop Books is an imprint of Bright Mountain Books, Inc.

Printed in the United States of America

ISBN-10: 0-914875-53-1
ISBN-13: 978-0-914875-53-6

CONTENTS

John Henry Moss

BASEBALL'S MIRACLE MAN

Chapter 1
REBIRTH OF A BASEBALL LEAGUE

John Henry Moss has had two public passions in life. Working as mayor of historic Kings Mountain, North Carolina, gave him great satisfaction for twenty-four years. His other passion was the game of baseball, in which he spent more than a half century organizing and operating minor leagues that furnished promising players to the major leagues.

Since his first endeavor in baseball in 1948, John Moss brought the professional game to more North Carolina cities and towns than any other person, living or dead. He also brought baseball to cities in New Jersey, Kentucky, South Carolina, Georgia, West Virginia, Maryland, and Ohio.

He was the architect and father of the Western Carolina League in 1948, becoming the youngest league president in baseball, and, after an eleven-year hiatus, operated that league, which later became the present-day South Atlantic League, for five decades. He worked with some of the finest minds ever in Major League Baseball, and helped such small Tar Heel towns as Newton, Conover, Shelby, Forest City, Marion, Gastonia, Hendersonville, and even tiny Belmont. All profited by linking their fortunes with those of John Moss and bringing professional baseball into their ballparks.

Twice Moss was called on to organize the Western Carolina League, at one time one of the nation's leading Class D leagues, and twice he responded, first in 1948 and again in 1959. He served continuously as president of the league through 2007 before becoming president emeritus in 2008. The job he did in reorganizing the league in 1959 for the 1960 season was considered textbook work in the minds of baseball men everywhere. The story is a classic example of how baseball worked in the old days and of the value of a handshake between honorable men, something seldom seen in baseball today.

This was the way baseball worked at that time:

Men who had the means to finance minor league baseball clubs came to John Moss in the fall of 1959 and asked him to reorganize the Western Carolina League, which had been defunct since it collapsed financially in 1952, five years after Moss had originally organized it for the 1948 season. After the necessary preliminaries of locating eight club owners and towns willing to join the league, John Moss made sure they had sufficient stadiums, personnel, and potential drawing power to operate on the Class D level. He then he turned his attention to finding ballplayers. In those days, that meant securing working agreements with major league teams for each club. A working agreement was simply a contract between major and minor league clubs which stipulated that the majors would furnish finances as well as ballplayers whose skills needed honing, to minor league teams. In return, the minor leagues would develop the players sufficiently to play in the major leagues.

Known as the farm system, the program had been developed by Branch Rickey, owner of the St. Louis Cardinals, in 1935. It reached such proportions after World War II that Rickey, who then owned and operated the Brooklyn Dodgers, furnished players and money to thirty-three minor league teams—one more than enough to field four eight-team leagues.

It was to Rickey that John Henry Moss eventually turned in 1959 when the American and National leagues rejected his plea for help.

George M. Trautman, president of the National Association of Professional Baseball Leagues, Inc. (later called the National Association of Minor League Baseball), with whom Moss had built a friendship when he originally organized the Western Carolina League in 1948, invited John to St. Petersburg, Florida, for the baseball Winter Meetings in December of 1959. Trautman promised Moss an audience with major league farm directors in an attempt to secure working agreements.

Moss met with the farm directors on a Sunday morning. Trautman introduced him. "Gentlemen, John wants to present the eight clubs he has in the reformed Western Carolina League for your consideration for working agreements." He beckoned Moss to the podium and continued, "John, tell 'em about it." Trautman had been a colonel in the army during World War II and expressed himself with authority. Moss made the presentation with a concise description of the eight towns in his league, their stadiums, and all other pertinent information the farm directors needed.

Trautman returned to the podium and said, "Now, fellows, you've heard the presentation, and I know that John has a good league. He first put this league together in 1947 and 1948 and operated it successfully as long as he ran it. He is a well-known man who knows the right people in his area. It's going to be a good Class D league." He looked at each of the farm directors and then said, "Those who would like to talk about putting working agreements in the Western Carolina League, hold up your hands."

No hands went up. John Moss had suspected that might happen. Because of what he had learned about organization and operation in the army during the war, and after having worked in both professional baseball and football as a minor league president and general manager, he was not overwhelmed by the negative response. He was not happy with it but still was not ready to fold his tent and steal away. Trautman, however, was surprised. After the meeting, he suggested that Moss return and make another presentation.

"It looks like you didn't do too well, John," Trautman said. "I'll tell you what: I'm going to have the farmers back here for a meeting Tuesday morning. Could you come back then and make another presentation—make up something different to tell 'em?"

"Yes, I'll be happy to come back," John said, "and I thank you for the invitation." He was a gentleman of the first order.

At the breakfast gathering on Tuesday, Trautman opened the meeting by saying, "I'm going to start off with John Moss making another presentation to you. I know you're all interested in hearing what he has to say, and I trust some of you have had conversions since Sunday."

John Henry spoke again about his league, adding rhetoric that he hadn't used at the Sunday meeting. Trautman returned to the podium and asked, "How many of you are convinced now that you ought to get in there with John in the Western Carolina League? Hold up your hands."

Again, no one raised a hand.

Moss returned to the podium. "Gentlemen, I thank you for the opportunity of making these presentations," he said, "but I'm here to tell you that the Western Carolina League is going to go, with you or without you. That, of course, is no threat—just a statement of fact—and having said that, I want to extend an invitation to you to join us at any time you feel we can help you. I know there are reasons why you can't help us now, including short notice, but you'll always be welcome in our ballparks. I want to reiterate that the Western Carolina League is going to play baseball next summer."

He turned to Trautman. "Mr. Trautman, I thank you for your kindness in having me here twice and for the fine breakfast this morning. And thank all of you for your time." John has always been a polite man with words.

After the meeting, Trautman confided, "John, we're always happy to have you. You're welcome here any time this office can be of assistance to the league. We particularly like the idea of a new league in North Carolina." He recalled the years when North Carolina had fielded more minor leagues and teams than any state in the union, including baseball-loving Texas and California, and that hundreds of ballplayers had made their way through the North Carolina leagues to the majors.

"Thank you very much, Mr. Trautman," John said, and he left.

Walking out of the meeting room to the hotel lobby, John's wheels were rolling. He knew that Branch Rickey, possibly the greatest baseball tactician ever, was working diligently in New York to build a third major league, the Continental League, so John shrugged and said to himself, "I may as well make a third presentation." No one ever accused John Moss of being shy where baseball was concerned.

He found a pay phone and from the operator got the number of the Continental League in New York City and dialed the league headquarters. Arthur Mann, a former New York sports writer who was then executive assistant to Rickey, answered the phone.

"This is John Moss calling from North Carolina," John said. "I want to speak with Mr. Rickey."

Over the line, John heard Mann say in hushed tones, "Mr. Rickey, John Moss down in North Carolina wants to speak to you," and heard Rickey say to put him on the line.

John said, "Mr. Rickey, I'm John Moss, president of the Western Carolina League. We have eight cities ready to play baseball. All of them have been in professional baseball before, and I believe we have put together a good league."

"What are the cities, John?"

"We have Lexington, Salisbury, Hickory, Newton-Conover, Shelby, Rutherford County, Statesville, and Gastonia."

"Well, I've been in every one of them," Rickey said, and John heard him say aside to Arthur Mann, "Arthur, John's wanting to talk to me about the Western Carolina League. He has eight cities down there, and I've been in all of them. Good baseball territory."

"Mr. Rickey," John said, "what I'd like to do is come up and sit down with you and lay out a program to let you know about the facilities and owners and the operations of our clubs. I really believe it will be a good league. I'd like to come Thursday."

"Arthur, what are we doing Thursday? John wants to come up to New York."

"Let me see, Mr. Rickey." A pause, then, "We're due in Toronto Thursday."

"Can't do it Thursday, John," Rickey said. "We're going to be in Toronto."

"How about Monday, Mr. Rickey?"

"Arthur, John said he can come up on Monday. Can we meet him here?"

"Yes," Arthur said, "we're clear in the afternoon."

Rickey: "John, could you be here at four o'clock Monday afternoon? Room 700, Canada Building."

"Yes, sir, Mr. Rickey, I'll be there."

Moss returned to his home in Kings Mountain and immediately booked a flight out of Charlotte to New York for the following Monday. After checking into a hotel when he arrived in New York, he rode a cab to the Canada Building, arriving in the offices of the Continental League at four o'clock sharp.

Inside the suite, no one was at the reception desk to greet him, but he heard voices coming from an adjoining room. He knocked on the door and went in.

Inside the room were Rickey, truly an icon of baseball to whose face almost everyone tendered respect by calling him Mr. Rickey; Arthur Mann; Arthur Davis of the family that donated the Davis Cup to tennis, an investor in the Continental League; Charles A. Hurth, former president of the Southern Association; and Mrs. Joan W. Payson, who later bought the New York Mets.

Rickey spoke to them. "John has come up here to talk to us about affiliating with the eight clubs in the Western Carolina League. He has eight teams in North Carolina, and I've been to all his cities and know them well. We're going to review the cities and facilities and the ownerships, and it is my opinion that we will certainly have considerable interest in this project."

Moss briefly presented his case, and the others showed interest, asking many questions. They had to have minor league teams to develop major league ballplayers, and John was the first to propose a feeder league. John Moss had more than his own rhetoric working for him. Rickey always had a soft spot in his heart for North Carolina, having operated and often visited in Asheville. As owner of the St. Louis Cardinals, Brooklyn Dodgers, and Pittsburgh Pirates, he had operated farm teams in Asheville, North Carolina, for more than a quarter century.

The discussion went on until 8:30 p.m. when Rickey looked at his watch and exclaimed, "We ought to have some food."

He directed the others. "You take John out and have a nice steak dinner. I will remain here, and Arthur, I want you to bring me an egg sandwich and a glass of milk."

Mrs. Payson excused herself. "If you don't mind, I have another place I must go."

"Oh, that will be all right, Mrs. Payson," Rickey said. "We'll fill you in."

They were gone an hour and a half, and only Arthur and John returned. As Rickey ate his egg sandwich, the discussion resumed and the three talked nonstop till 2:00 a.m. Finally, Rickey looked at his watch. "Arthur," he said, "let's go to the hotel. Get a cab."

Moss had engaged a room in the same hotel where Rickey and Mann stayed. He was on the eighth floor and they were higher. When the elevator stopped at the eighth, John said, "Mr. Rickey, we haven't concluded our arrangement yet. We haven't made a deal about what we're going to do. What time can we get together tomorrow?"

John stepped out of the elevator, held the door open, and stuck his head back in. "I expected to have something concrete to take back to North Carolina with me," he said. "Can we meet tomorrow, or rather later today, and conclude the deal?"

Rickey offered his hand and smiled. He said, "We have concluded the deal, John. I'll send you confirmation in writing."

The handshake proved to be worth more than a million dollars to the WCL. Few, if any, in baseball can recall a deal of that magnitude being confirmed with a handshake—and Rickey proved to be as good as his word.

John Moss never thought for a moment that he wouldn't be.

Chapter 2
THE CONTINENTAL LEAGUE

The Continental League provided a sound working agreement with the Western Carolina League. True to Rickey's word, the Continental League agreed to pay all of the Western Carolina League's managers' salaries and $100 monthly of all player salaries. In addition—and this was a major stroke—the Continental would provide all balls, bats, and uniforms for the WCL players. The uniforms were new, not like the used uniforms that American and National league clubs handed down to minor league affiliates. There were no established uniforms in the Continental League; the league was not in operation yet at the major league level.

The eight cities chosen for original membership in the Continental League were New York, Toronto, Buffalo, Dallas-Fort Worth, Houston, Atlanta, Minneapolis, and Denver. Rickey had chosen his cities well; he was a man far ahead of his time. Seven of the Continental League's eight cities—all except Buffalo—soon became major league cities, but in the American and National leagues rather than in the Continental.

Moss and Rickey matched a Continental League city with each of the WCL clubs. This maneuver got a lot of ink in the Continental League's cities, especially in New York. Reading all of this, without full explanation of how it was being structured, Ford Frick, commissioner of baseball, became concerned that Rickey and Moss were putting together a conglomerate that would pool ballplayers. Actually, Frick went beyond concern; he moved to assure that pooling wouldn't happen. He spent considerable time on the telephone with George Trautman and Moss and wasted a lot of postage writing Rickey. Actually, at no time did either Rickey or Moss advocate pooling of players. Their agreement was that each Western Carolina League team would work with one Continental League club.

"I had the season set to open May first of 1960," Moss said. "I was making the rounds of our league, working for Mr. Rickey inspecting ballparks that hadn't been used in four years. He was spending a lot of money with us and needed someone out of his office to take a look at ballparks. I was doing that for him. But in the meantime, I had our people putting together the same organizations they had previously had."

In March, the Eastern Regionals of the NCAA college basketball tournament were held in the Charlotte Coliseum. Eastern teams were involved, and the New York press gathered in Charlotte to cover them. Moss thought it would be expedient to hold a press conference in Charlotte for the benefit of the Continental and Western Carolina leagues. He set up the conference at the Hotel Charlotte and sent invitations to all local and New York press and to other Eastern newspapers to attend the press conference on Sunday, March 20.

The large room in which the press conference was held was crowded with newspaper and magazine writers, television crews, and radio jockeys. John Henry had been in Birmingham the previous day and had flown to Charlotte in choppy weather. Rickey had come down from New York.

Moss conducted the conference. He told the press what North Carolina cities were involved and explained their plans to be affiliated with the Continental League. He introduced Rickey and said he would cover the relationship between the two leagues and answer any questions.

Rickey made brief opening remarks and asked for questions. This was an opportunity the press, particularly the New York press, had been waiting for. The first man who jumped to his feet to ask a question was Dick Young, the spirited sports columnist for the *New York Daily News*. "Mr. Rickey," he asked, "where are you going to get ballplayers?"

Rickey tucked his tongue firmly in his cheek and answered Young. "Where are we going to get ballplayers? Why, John has more ballplayers than we have uniforms." That was a true statement, since the Continental League had no uniforms at all.

"To be more precise," he continued, "we met three potential players on our way in from the airport to the hotel. One was a young man who brought our car up at the car rental place, and we stopped at a convenience store and met a young man who might be a ballplayer, and then when we checked in here at the hotel the young fellow who carried our luggage up was a potential player—if he can play baseball.

"That's where we're going to get ballplayers, Mr. Young—wherever we find them, just the way the present major leagues get theirs. We had sixteen major league clubs when we were a nation of 110 million people or less, and today we have 200 million Americans, and yet you wonder where we're going to get ballplayers?"

Red Smith, sports columnist for the *New York Herald-Tribune*, stood in the back of the room grinning like a cheshire cat at Rickey's adroit handling of Dick Young. Red then asked, "Branch, I agree that you're right that there are ballplayers out there. Tell me how you're going to affect this and keep Ford Frick happy."

"Oh well, Mr. Smith," Rickey replied, "John and I will formulate a plan that will meet the guidelines of baseball and hopefully meet Mr. Frick's requirements. He'll be proud of it, I feel sure."

Rickey went through all eight cities of the Continental League and spoke of each owner.

"Now most of you fellows know who Adolph Coors is. He's in the brewery business in Denver, and he will be president of that club. Up at Toronto is Charles Bronfman; he's in the spirits business. You all know that I don't partake of spirits, but I understand the business he's in. Over in Buffalo is Ralph Wilson. He's in the football business, and we feel certain he will be capable of handling baseball too. Judge Roy Hofheinz and Bob Smith are in Houston. They're reputable men. If Judge Hofheinz was here today, I'd have to sit down and let him talk."

Rickey delivered his comments with a note of mirth in his voice, and the press ate it up.

"Mr. Whitman of Minneapolis—" Rickey said, "his family has been in the farm implement business for years. Stable citizens!"

He went on in that manner until he had the press firmly in his hand. "My whole career," he concluded, "has been built around having confidence in good men."

Like Branch Rickey, John Henry Moss had learned to place

confidence in capable men, a stroke through which he would profit immensely later, but he had had to go through a bloody world war to learn that lesson.

Moss began the press conference at one o'clock and it lasted until three. "Mr. Rickey," he said later, "was a phenomenally charming man."

Chapter 3
THE WESTERN CAROLINA LEAGUE

Unfortunately for both Moss and Rickey, the Continental League didn't get off the ground; it never cleared the runway. But the Western Carolina League did. It had a tremendous season in 1960. A few years later, for three seasons it was classified as the leading Class D league in baseball, in operation, attendance, and other considerations.

After that press conference in Charlotte and before the Continental League folded, John Moss sat down with Branch Rickey and Arthur Mann and worked out arrangements for spring training. Since the league had not scheduled opening day until May 1, training in Florida was not good business. April weather in Piedmont North Carolina is fit for baseball, so they decided to have spring training at home. Two training sites were set up, one in Gastonia and the other in Newton-Conover, two towns near Hickory that jointly shared a team.

As Rickey had explained to Dick Young at the press conference, in a roundabout way, the league had no trouble coming up with more than enough ballplayers to put presentable Class D baseball on its diamonds.

"We ran advertisements for ballplayers all over the league," Moss explained. "Applications flowed in from kids who wanted a chance, from farm boys, from capable college players, and from former professional players who felt they could still play the game."

Team managers had been hired, most with professional managerial or player experience: Jack Hale at Lexington, Larry Taylor at Salisbury, Joe Abernethy in Hickory, John Isaac at Newton-Conover, Rube Wilson at Shelby, Jim Poole in Rutherford County, Jake Early in Statesville, and Billy Queen at Gastonia. They were men who knew the game of baseball inside and out, and all were good baseball teachers, a requisite for managing minor league teams.

Rickey came down from New York for spring training, giving John Moss double duty; he had to chauffeur Rickey around as well as tend to his duties as league president. "That was one of the highlights of my career," John Henry said. "I have already said what a charming fellow Mr. Rickey was, and he was also a good baseball man, actually a great baseball man. He really knew the intricacies of the game." Rickey had been a major league catcher-outfielder for three seasons and had worked in baseball for most of his life.

Rickey brought some brilliant baseball minds with him to work with players at the spring training camps, including Burt Shotten, who had managed eleven years in the majors. In a four-year stint with Rickey's Dodgers, Shotten's team had won pennants in 1947 and 1949, losing the World Series to the power-laden New York Yankees both times. Rickey also brought Clyde Sukeforth, who had played ten years with Cincinnati and Brooklyn; and Al Todd, an eleven-year veteran with the Philadelphia Phillies, Pittsburgh Pirates, Brooklyn Dodgers, and Chicago Cubs.

They alternated between the training sites, spending two days in Newton-Conover and two in Gastonia. "Our managers and I had pretty good assistants in spring training," Moss recalled with a laugh. "We moved Burt Shotten and his wife into quarters in the Kings Mountain Public Library, where several upstairs rooms were used for housing teachers, and we put Sukeforth and Todd in a motel in Gastonia.

"Mr. Rickey would have me drive them here and there, and I would sit with them at training sessions and wherever they went. We went up to Salisbury one night to see an exhibition game at old Newman Park where Catawba College played. Mr. Rickey and Shotten had both had recent cataract operations on their eyes, and in batting practice, someone was hitting balls up against an old metal outfield fence. I could hear them hit the fence—Whap! Whap!— but I couldn't follow the flight of the ball.

"Shotten would say, 'Boy, that ball was hit sharp, Branch,' and Mr. Rickey would say, 'Yes, it was. He hit it on a line.' I didn't know whether they were putting me on or not, but I suspect they also had trouble following the ball and were trying to convince me of how great their eyesight was after surgery.

"They could kid me all they wanted to, but from them I learned a lot about baseball, and much about people, and more about the history of baseball. That year I probably spent ninety days with Mr. Rickey, driving him to games, taking him to speak to civic clubs, and here and there for other reasons. Great experience!" Rickey was a famous man and civic clubs were thrilled to have a speaker of his caliber.

"Spring training stocked the Western Carolina League clubs with fine players," Moss said, "and we got the league off to a good start. We were happy to have the money the Continental League put into our clubs. It helped us make that good start."

Unfortunately, the Continental League ran into a couple of roadblocks it could not pass. Rickey and his cohorts had the league almost ready to go when the American and National leagues dug in to stop it.

The missing link in the Continental League's makeup was a national television contract. Rickey put Bronfman, Hofheinz, Coors, and a New York consultant on a committee to develop a television program, intending to use network influence to get sponsorships for

Moss presents Greenville team president Verner Ross with the Western Carolinas League championship flag for the 1970 season. The Greenville Red Sox won the crown with a regular-season record of 77–52.

telecasts, and they were making progress. Coors had gotten a third of the necessary sponsorships, Rickey had secured a quarter of one sponsorship, and Bronfman was close to arranging one.

Rickey had John Moss come to his New York office for a couple of days, and Moss was present when Adolph Coors came into Rickey's office and said, "Now, Branch, you've got to get our sponsorships tied down. We need to get these people together and sign contracts. I have to go back to Denver this afternoon, and we will get this wrapped up next week. Then there won't be a damned thing the major leagues can do except watch us play baseball."

"That's the last we ever saw of Mr. Coors," John Moss said. "He disappeared on his way home and has never been found."

While Rickey was still working on the Continental League, the major leagues reached a decision to expand, possibly to thwart efforts of the Continental League. The New York Giants and the Brooklyn Dodgers had moved their franchises to California before the start of the 1958 season, signaling a chain of events that led to Major League Baseball's first expansion in sixty years. The American League made its first move in 1960, enlarging itself to ten teams for the 1961 season.

So the two things that contributed most to the fold-up of the Continental League were the disappearance of Coors, which took away a vital financial commitment to the Continental League, and expansion of the major leagues. Without the promised franchises of those four cities, the Continental League quietly closed its doors and went out of business.

"Choosing the expansion cities was not easy for either major league," John Moss said. "I was in Washington for a dinner to cel-ebrate the 100th year of professional baseball in 1961 at the same time of the meeting to choose the four expansion teams.

"Several of us were talking in a corner on the mezzanine when one of those who had applied for an expansion franchise and lost emerged from the meeting and violently flung his briefcase against the wall. It burst open and scattered papers around the hallway. We learned a few minutes later that Houston had been chosen in his place. He kept walking and his aides retrieved and repacked the briefcase."

John Henry concluded, "Baseball probably saw that the day was near, and it had enough inside information to know that the only reason there wasn't already a third major league that the current majors would support, was because there had been no one to organize it. The success of any major sport now requires television and radio contracts. The Continental owners recognized that, but didn't have time to get their ducks in a row before the major leagues beat them to it."

Why, the question has always nagged, instead of enlarging the American and National leagues to unmanageable proportions, didn't the major leagues have Rickey place his Continental League under the aegis of Major League Baseball? No good answer was ever offered.

That was the demise of the Continental League. When it folded, its payments to the WCL were cut off. "We overcame that by tightening our belts a little," John Moss said, "and by developing the operational capacities of the ownerships. Players signed under our agreement with the Continental League were the property of the Western Carolina League teams, and we had the uniforms and bats and balls that were left over from the Continental League's demise. About all we had to pick up were the salaries of our managers and the $100 the Continental was paying each of our players, plus umpires salaries."

The WCL had conducted its own umpire's school in Newton, and had come out of it with enough men to umpire the league's games. John Sherrill and Johnny Shives, veteran minor league umpires, had run the school. Because of that effort the league didn't have to go to the expense of advertising for umpires. Sports department personnel of the league's newspapers, plus the nearby Charlotte, Winston-Salem, and Asheville papers, ran stories on the league's umpiring school, and player and umpiring candidates emerged from all over the league's area and beyond.

Chapter 4
GROWING UP IN KINGS MOUNTAIN

As a lad, growing up in the 1930s in Kings Mountain, North Carolina, John Henry Moss had no choice but to learn to love baseball. His father, Manual A. Moss, known by his initials M. A., was a spectacular baseball pitcher who threw ambidextrously, pitching equally well with either arm.

When he pitched, he caused much discussion and often consternation among opposing teams and fans. He pitched right-handed to right-handed batters and left-handed to left-handed batters, forcing his breaking pitches to slide away from hitters. Many of M. A.'s contemporaries, including his brothers, told John later that his father was an unusually skilled pitcher.

He never pitched professionally because he made a good living in the textile business, the lifeblood of Kings Mountain. He installed textile machinery, which required almost as much skill as throwing a baseball left- or right-handed. Textile machinery had to be set up correctly and fully balanced to make it function smoothly. Thus, M. A. Moss got his baseball kicks on the mounds of industrial teams in and around the Concord area of North Carolina and, for short periods of time, on the semipro mounds of New England, where he was often sent to install machinery in textile plants.

M. A.'s wife, Amanda Oates Moss, died in childbirth while bringing John into the world. She had given birth to two previous children, both girls. After her death, John went to live with his grandparents, William Henry (W. H.) Moss and Margaret Rippy Moss, in Kings Mountain, while M. A. worked at his textile job. John's sisters lived with an aunt in Kings Mountain for a couple of years, and when their father remarried they went to live with him, but John remained with his grandparents.

John's grandfather, W. H., was also in the textile business, but in a different capacity. He was a skilled carpenter who had moved from the Buffalo Community of Cleveland County to Kings Mountain in 1880, and there he had specialized as a subcontractor, framing big timbers for textile mills. At this writing, some of the mills he constructed are still standing and in full use.

"My grandfather had great ability," John Moss said. "It is amazing to see how those mills were constructed then, without steel, with only timbers, and how strong and sturdy they were. It taught me that baseball leagues had to be run as meticulously in order to gain results."

John's grandmother Margaret, who was reared in the Earl Community of Cleveland County, was a kindly woman who taught John Christian principles and made sure he had enough chores to do to become accustomed to work. She also encouraged him to do the very best he could in school and at any job or chore. John's Moss grandparents had a large family, and John stayed busy. He maintained a good family relationship with sisters, uncles, aunts, and cousins.

John's other grandparents were John James Oates and Cornelia Josephine Rohm Oates. John Henry was named for both of his grandfathers: John for his maternal grandpa and Henry for his paternal grandfather. He had very little relationship with his Oates grandparents who lived variously in Gaston and Lincoln counties where John Oates was active in the logging industry and moved around a lot.

John's early education came at Park Grace Grammar School, named for two textile mills in the area, and his higher education was at Kings Mountain High School. He did not play high school football or basketball. Quite naturally, partially because of his father's athletic ability, and because of the abundance of industrial teams in the area, his interests lay in baseball. In his senior year, he played second base on the Kings Mountain Junior American Legion team. He was a good glove-no hit infielder who could always find a place to play at that level because of his fielding skills.

After graduation from Kings Mountain High in 1938, John Henry worked for his father as a supervisor in textile machinery installation, a job that he calls "very small." He also played semi-pro baseball for the Park Yarns Mill team in Kings Mountain. His introduction to front-office work in baseball began there as manager of the Park Yarns team, a job in which he learned to work with players, and raising sponsorship money. He was also on the league's schedule-making committee, and there he learned that scheduling baseball games for an entire league was not the easiest job he had ever tackled.

Later he played with textile teams in the nearby Greenville, South Carolina, area. "I still couldn't hit any better," he said, "but if a team needed somebody who could catch and throw, I was their man."

Thus, his great love for every phase of baseball was born.

Chapter 5
WORLD WAR II: A TIME OF LEARNING

A year after John Moss was graduated from high school, Europe and parts of Asia flamed with war. Hitler's juggernauts murderously advanced in all directions from their homeland, and war clouds drifted westward across the Atlantic and hovered along America's eastern shore.

Three-and-a-half months before the December 7, 1941, Japanese bombing of Pearl Harbor, John Henry Moss was drafted into the U.S. Army. War appeared to be imminent in both directions, east and west, when he took the oath of service on the twenty-first of August 1941, at Fort Bragg, North Carolina. Two days later he was sent for basic training to Camp Croft, near Spartanburg, South Carolina, only thirty-five miles from his home in Kings Mountain.

The weekend he got to Camp Croft, John became a member of a training battalion baseball team. He arrived in August at the end of the season, and during that weekend the team had several games to play in Spartanburg's Duncan Park against local mill teams. John played second base and gave a good account with his glove but found that he still couldn't hit.

Basic training consumed fourteen weeks of his army career, and upon completion early in December 1941, about the time the Japanese almost annihilated America's Pacific Fleet at Pearl Harbor, launching the United States into World War II, John was assigned to Company I of the 113th Regiment of the 44th Infantry Division. That division was on maneuvers near Fort Bragg, and John reported for duty on the day the maneuvers ended.

The 113th headed north, arriving in Charlottesville, Virginia, on a Sunday afternoon, and John and several friends attended a tennis tournament that evening. The 44th Division assembled at Fort Dix, New Jersey, and almost immediately dispatched a group of troops to Island Heights, New York, to be housed on the John Wanamaker estate. Along with special units of the Coast Guard, the Navy, and the Army Air Corps, John became affiliated with the Eastern Defense Command, and was designated for special service.

Early in 1942, John's unit was attached to the Coast Guard and remained on Long Island to begin both classroom and field training for the defense of America's shores. During that year, John Henry played baseball and football on the Eastern Defense Command teams. Playing second base in baseball, John again wielded a rather hitless bat but managed to stay on the team because of his good glove. He was a punt returner in football.

"Being a member of both of those teams," John said, "was something of a tradeoff. A fellow on the football team told me he would get me on the team if I could get him on the baseball team, and when we were both successful we managed to escape a lot of rather rigorous physical training. I had never played football, but all I had to do was catch punts and run the ball back as fast and as far as I could."

In late 1942, an unusual opportunity arose for John. The army enrolled him to take business administration courses at New York University. "I took all sorts of business courses," John said, "and remained there until our units were broken up in 1944 and were sent overseas to the European theater of operations." At NYU John studied accounting, budgeting, record keeping, and other business-associated courses that would help a young man entering baseball office work, as John later did upon discharge.

He remained at NYU for a year and a half until classes were broken up soon after D-Day, the Allies' June 6, 1944, invasion of Continental Europe, and then was among those sent to Europe as replacement troops.

Landing in Normandy at La Haye-du-Puits, John was attached to Headquarters Company of the 79th Infantry Division. He was issued a tommy gun and .45 caliber automatic pistol and assigned as bodyguard to Gen. Frank Greer, brigadier of the 79th. After three months with General Greer, he was elevated to the position of bodyguard for Maj. Gen. Ira T. Wyche, a North Carolinian commanding the 79th Division—and there began a great education in dealing with superiors and subordinates. He remained with General

Wyche, who was soon promoted to commander of the XXth Corps, until the end of the war, and returned home to Kings Mountain on October 2, 1945, with Honorable Discharge in hand.

"I became a guy walking around trying to look sharp and smart and all that stuff," John said. "Being bodyguard for the corps commander, I had to remain close to him day and night until the war ended. This gave me great exposure to leadership capability and planning. We met with other corps commanders and on other occasions with collective groups of generals and commanders of various divisions, and I learned something at every meeting. It was like the Secret Service staying with the president night and day. We pitched our tent beside General Wyche's tent every night, and the only difference was that the general had a better tent."

Soon after his attachment to General Greer, John Moss thought he had become star-struck. In a stone building in a small French town—whose name John has long-since forgotten—General Greer was among the hierarchy of the 79th who met with generals Omar N. Bradley, George Patton, Ira Wyche, Bernard Montgomery, and their aides, to debate strategy.

"That was the first time I had seen General Patton—Old Blood and Guts, but I had the opportunity to observe him, even in action, several times after that. It was about Patton that someone later remarked, 'He was our greatest general since Sergeant York!'

"When I saw him that first time, we were getting ready to break out of Falaise Gap to make a run toward Reims," John said. "Before the battle began, I saw General Patton again, wearing those ivory-handled six-shooters and leading his dog on a leash. We met him in a field where the grain had been cut. He flew in on a small L-5 with his chauffeur, an aide, his dog, and the pilot. We couldn't believe there were four men in that L-5, but we discovered that when Patton wanted to do something, he did it, and that day he wanted three passengers in the plane with the pilot. I am sure Patton's chauffeur, who was from Forest City, North Carolina, was as starry-eyed as I from seeing all that brass. Patton always kept his chauffeur with him, this time because the chauffeur had driven him to the airport from which they took off, and he wanted the chauffeur with him when they returned.

"During that meeting in the field, I remember General Patton getting out a map and pointing to it and saying, 'Ira (referring to General Wyche), I know damned well you can handle this,' and General Wyche said, 'Oh yes, George.' Patton was making the rounds to see that commanding officers were ready for the push."

The next time John saw Patton, the American forces had smashed through the Gap and were in an area where Patton put the 5th Armored Division into combat. The Germans made a little run at the Americans and were doing some damage with their Messerschmidts.

John recalls Patton talking with a major, a big, nice-looking guy, of whom John said, "I'd bet my shirttail he was from Georgia Tech," but facing Patton the major spoke with mush in his mouth.

"Major," Patton commanded, "get in that goddamned tank and get it moving across that bridge."

The major responded, "General, I've got a man up there now trying to determine about explosives. I don't want these tanks to be blown up and stop our whole convoy."

Patton was obviously worried that the bridge would get knocked out, and it was the only way to get his tanks across the Saar River. He rapped his stick on the tank and said, "Get in this damned tank. I'll go on up there myself." The major got in the tank and Patton walked to the bridge. A couple of shells came in and the Messerschmidts were strafing, and Patton leaned against a tank, watching the aircraft.

Where was John Moss when this occurred? "I'll tell you where I was," he said. "I was in a ditch. He could go up there if he wanted to. I didn't know where General Wyche was. I think they were back behind us somewhere."

Patton walked forward and observers told him the German explosives fixed to the bridge had been disarmed by a nine-year-old kid who was almost electrocuted when he pulled the wires loose.

"We rolled from there toward Paris," John said, "and one day Gen. George C. Marshall was there, and I was in charge of security. That was a pretty big thing for me. I enjoyed it and learned a lot about command and management in general, seeing things and making decisions."

On that day when Marshall was present, the 113th bogged down in a little French town and had to fight door to door. A tank destroyer unit, armed with heavy guns, had been attached to the infantry commanded by General Greer. Growing impatient with the street fighting, General Greer commanded, "Let's bring that TD up here and see if it can knock that damned wall down and get them Krauts out of there."

The tank destroyer fired two quick rounds and down came the wall. German troops charged out, running and scattering, trying to elude death or capture. They were firing on the run, and the American units engaged them, capturing some and killing others while a few escaped.

"We had a terrible time getting through that town," John said. "We had to knock holes in almost every wall we came to, or else bring them down entirely, and the farther we went, the less the Germans wanted to fight. Soon, many of them surrendered, and after that we drove on through the town, headed for Paris."

Perhaps subconsciously, John Moss remembered and filed in his mind the things he saw that would help him in future endeavors. He saw a tremendous amount of ingenuity on the part of American unit commanders. "I'll never forget a Texan named Olin Teague," he said. "He was a lieutenant colonel, a battalion commander who was later elected to congress. Teague, with the help of an engineering battalion, put a bridge across the Saar River that enabled Patton to roll his tanks across and cut off a segment of the German army, about one hundred thousand men.

"Time and time again, I saw things like that," John added, "things that made me know that if you took a leadership role over good men, you could accomplish what you wanted. It was a privilege to see that happening all over the battlefront at that level. At the time, I thought it was the kind of thing a businessman, or perhaps a baseball executive, would need to know."

March 24, 1945, was a day that John Moss has never forgotten. Secure in a little bungalow outside St. Lo, near Verdun, the site of heavy fighting in both World Wars, John was in charge of bodyguards welcoming Gen. Dwight D. Eisenhower, the Supreme Allied Commander, for a strategy conference.

"In late afternoon I was sitting in a swing on the porch of our bungalow," John said. "I was enjoying the first sun we'd seen in a while and having trouble staying awake. Suddenly a noise came down the street and General Eisenhower's entourage approached. One of Ike's boys led the press corps into the yard first, and in a minute a command car rolled up and General Eisenhower stepped out. I jumped up and saluted him and about that time General Wyche came out on the porch.

"Ike said to him, 'Well, general, you're looking pretty good.' General Wyche returned, 'Thank you, general.'"

Eisenhower had come for a 7:00 p.m. meeting, and it was dark by the time the group finished gathering. John and some of the other bodyguards "counted stars"—those on the shoulders of the numerous generals present—and came up with forty-four.

Generals Omar N. Bradley, George C. Marshall, Jacob L. Devers, Anthony C. McAuliffe, Montgomery, Patton, and several others were there. McAuliffe was commander of the 101st Airborne Division, and while defending Bastogne during the Battle of the Bulge, it was he whose troops beat down a German counterattack and then in reply to a terse Nazi ultimatum to surrender, sent back the famous reply, "Nuts!" Devers also distinguished himself. Commander of the Sixth Army Group, made up of American and French forces, Devers cleared Alsace, crossed the Rhine, and swept through Germany to the Swiss border.

"I don't remember whether Gen. Bedell Smith was there," Moss said, "but there were many, and I mean many, men present with stars on their shoulders, commanders and their aides. For an hour and a half, they formed strategy for the final push against the Nazis."

John had orders that *nobody* was to step on the porch of that bungalow. Armed with the tommy gun and .45 automatic pistol, he had two other guards on the porch and a tight perimeter guard around the bungalow.

Germany capitulated on May 8, 1945, and the war in Europe ended, but fighting still raged in the Pacific. General Wyche was commander of the XXth Corps, and one day soon after the end of the war, Wyche and Moss and some others went over to G2 headquarters to review a parade. Standing on the reviewing stand,

General Wyche turned to John and said, "I'm going to be speaking to fifteen or twenty thousand troops, and I'm trying to get my thoughts together. I want to ask you what would be your greatest aspirations for returning to America."

"Well, I think I'll need a while to give that some thought, sir," John said.

"All right," the general returned. "I'm going over here and will be back in a few minutes, so start thinking."

He sounded like my daddy, John thought.

When the general returned, he said, "John, what are your thoughts?"

"Well, general," John began, "if the Lord will give me good health, I'll make it the rest of the way on my own."

"That's good," said the general, and a few minutes later he came to John again, and said, "I'll be going to the Pacific to see Doug (MacArthur). You want to go with me?"

"Thank you, sir," John responded immediately, "but I believe I'll get off in Kings Mountain."

Later, when John returned home, he read that General Wyche had been made Inspector General of the Army.

In retrospect, Moss considers his four years of service in the army during World War II as time well spent. "The army was an integral part of my life," he said. "The training, the opportunity to attend NYU, and all the administrative courses I took were very helpful to me in later life. Being with General Wyche gave me a broad perspective of what was going on, so I could better appreciate the things I saw, the experiences I had, and the things I learned. The opportunity to meet men like General Patton and General Vandenberg, commander of the 9th Air Force, brought me to realize the value of the order of command—which, of course, anyone in a responsible job should know."

Chapter 6
GLORY DAYS

Glory days immediately followed the cessation of hostilities in August of 1945. That was a time for rebuilding America in a new and different world. The relief everyone felt, having the war over, was as if an overcast had been blown from American skies by a strong gale, and everyone began to come out in the sunshine, looking for something. Most settled for entertainment.

There had been enough fighting, killing, and wounding. Five long years of mayhem in Europe and the Pacific—four involving the United States—made much of the populace forget what it was like to live in a peaceful world.

John Henry Moss returned to Kings Mountain that fall on the second of October, looking for a job. He met some friends he had known as youngsters who had been in service, and all were casting around for something to do.

John and a fellow named Fred Dixon, whom John had known all his life, went into the concrete block business together. They sold blocks to building contractors in and around Kings Mountain and, in doing so, built a reputation with the church community.

"I didn't know what I was going to do for a career," John said. "We helped churches in Kings Mountain, Shelby, and Gastonia by selling them blocks, but I realized early in 1946 that it was going to be hard for me to stay out of baseball. Going to games as a fan wasn't satisfying enough, so as spring approached I organized the Kings Mountain Vets semipro baseball team and entered a textile league with other teams in Gastonia, Mount Holly, and Mecklenburg County. We played games twice a week and had reasonably good success in a pretty good league."

The league was expanded to include Shelby, Valdese, and Cherryville in 1947, and increased its playing schedule to four games a week. The league was exceptionally strong that year. Ballplayers were paid for games played, a carryover from the old semipro days of the 1930s.

"Applying to baseball the basic business traits I had learned in the army," Moss said, "we had a decent year in a very good league." All those business courses at NYU, the leadership qualities he had learned from army brass, the delegation of authority to capable subordinates, the qualities of management and command he had studied while watching superiors make life-and-death decisions in the heat of combat, observing how good men can rise to any occasion in leadership roles, and knowing and adhering to the order of command—all these qualities gave him a broad perspective that he realized more every day could be applied to baseball. If ever a man had received an education in military service, he was the man.

"I learned much in the army that helped me later, just by plain observation," Moss said. "We were working under rather serious conditions. People were dying."

John Henry's knowledge of baseball grew vastly when he added what he learned working with Branch Rickey. "Who better than Branch Rickey," he asked himself, "to walk into baseball with? That was phenomenal training for the tasks ahead. One of the major lessons I learned from him was never to be overbearing, but also having no problem telling others what I wanted them to do."

As summer progressed, John came to the conclusion that his blood was thickening with baseball to the extent that it would never thin again.

Fortified with these qualities, John was not surprised when a delegation of businessmen from various small North Carolina towns came to him early in 1948 and asked if he could lead them into professional baseball in a new league they wanted him to organize.

They were men of enough means to finance minor league baseball teams. Most were people who had been affiliated with semipro teams in the western and Piedmont sections of North Carolina, and obviously recognizing Moss's skill and expertise from the way he ran his semipro team, they thought he would be the man to put them into professional baseball.

Arranging a meeting with John, they put the league together with towns already committed: Forest City, Lenoir, Lincolnton,

Marion, Morganton, Newton and Conover together, and Shelby. One place remained to be filled, and John secured Hendersonville to complete the league. The name chosen for the league was the Western Carolina League, meaning the western part of North Carolina, where all eight teams were located. Years later when South Carolina towns came into the league, it became plural as the Western Carolinas League.

The Western Carolina League's ownership was solid. The men involved were good businessmen and upstanding citizens in their communities. C. O. Ridings of Forest City, that team's business manager, later became a congressman. T. Lee Osborne owned the Cadillac agency in Hendersonville. Earl H. Tate had been mayor of Lenoir for thirty years. In Marion, the team was headed by men like Otis L. Broyhill, president, a member of the famous Broyhill furniture family; Hugh Beam, secretary-treasurer, superintendent of McDowell County Schools; and J. C. Rabb, business manager, who was a member of the North Carolina General Assembly. Morganton's president, J. W. Beach, was an outstanding citizen; secretary-treasurer H. L. Riddle was a physician, and business manager Boger McGimsey was the team's first baseman, and a good one too.

All of the league's other owners and operators were fine people. Moss either knew them personally or knew of them, and he was happy with the league's executive personnel. The team owners then hired managers and chose names for the clubs.

The Forest City Owls would be managed by Gene Hollifield, a catcher who had played in the International League; the Hendersonville Skylarks by Charlie Munday, the veteran professional and semipro catcher who had managed many semipro teams; the Lenoir Red Sox by Claude A. Jonnard, a six-year veteran of the major leagues with the New York Giants, St. Louis Browns, and Chicago White Sox, who had pitched in the 1923 and 1924 World Series for the Giants, first against the Yankees and then against the Senators of Walter Johnson's day; the Lincolnton Cardinals by Fred Withers; the Marion Marauders by Wes Ferrell, who had racked up a 193–128 pitching record with six major league clubs in fifteen years; Newton-Conover Twins by Eddie Yount, a player for the

Philadelphia Athletics and the Pirates in the 1930s; and the Shelby Farmers by Rube Wilson.

Wilson was from Hickory, in the midst of WCL territory, and was a great addition to the league. He had played and managed in independent and professional leagues from Class AA down to Class D. He was an image manager and a baseball personality who had played the game for a long time. Moss soon discovered that Rube wielded considerable influence in the league and that his influence was entirely wholesome. After he quit managing a few years later, Wilson continued on in baseball, mostly as a scout, until the mid-1990s. Both his career and influence contributed to an illustrious stretch for Rube in Minor League Baseball in the Southeastern United States.

"That was a collection of great managers," Moss said. "I don't know if I could handle them today or not. Most were playing managers and all had independent ideas about how to play the game."

The league's towns ranged in size from Lincolnton's population of 6,500 to Hendersonville's 17,000 and Shelby's 18,000. The

John Henry Moss (second from right) discusses the new Western Carolina League in 1948 with (left to right) Robert L. Finch, public relations director of the National Association; Hal Weafer, director of the National Association umpires; and Clyde A. Short, president of the Shelby Farmers Baseball Club.

Fairgrounds in Hendersonville was the league's largest park, with a 5,000 seating capacity. Marion owned the second largest stadium with 4,000 seats. The others ranged downward to Morganton's 2,000, and all were sufficient for Class D baseball.

"We began organizational efforts in October of 1947," John Henry said, "and had the league together in time to attend the baseball Winter Meetings in Miami in December."

Finding enough baseballs to play a season was one of the league's biggest problems, apparently due to a scarcity of horsehide in those immediate postwar days and also to the number of minor leagues in baseball's rapidly expanding structure. At a meeting in Columbus, Ohio, the Western Carolina was welcomed into the minor league family. With the help of George Trautman, John got his league's baseballs at that meeting.

"Got them from MacGregor," John said. "Trautman told Phil Goldsmith, president of MacGregor Sporting Goods Company, to let me have the balls."

Goldsmith had just furnished the official football for the Rose Bowl, a stroke that was sure to increase sales of MacGregor balls. John and Trautman cornered Goldsmith after the meetings ended. "Listen here, Phil," Trautman said in the crisp tones of an army colonel, "find four hundred dozen baseballs for John."

"Well," said Phil, "you're riding down on the same train I am. Let's get off in Cincinnati and go over to the factory and work this out."

They made the deal, and the next day Moss caught the train that took him through Asheville and Spartanburg and on home to Kings Mountain. "Those baseballs took us almost through the season," John said. "We got some more before the season ended, but not nearly that many."

John encountered few problems in organizing the league, but there was one during the season that added greatly to the caliber of baseball played in the WCL. However, it eventually killed the league. That was the violation of salary limits.

The Western Carolina League had two restrictions: a seventeen-man roster for each team and a salary limit for each club of $2,600 a month. Salary limits were tough in those days, and in order to attract and obtain a core of veterans for each club, money was illegally being paid under the table. Every team in the league—actually, almost every team in Minor League Baseball—stretched its salary limit, some by large margins.

"There weren't supposed to be any exceptions," Moss said, "and the league presidents were kept in the dark." He chuckled when he said that. "But let us say that rumor had it that under-the-table payments to players were substantial in the WCL. Some players were paid as high as Triple-A salaries.

"We had people playing in the league with a lot of experience, like Phil Oates, who had just left the Giants camp, and others like Gene Hollifield and Eddie Yount, two of our playing managers who quit playing Triple-A for a chance to manage in our league. Hollifield and Yount were two that come to mind, and even old poker-faced Charlie Munday would pick up a bat and swing it at the plate every once in a while."

Working agreements in 1948 were limited. They were usually limited to portions of players. Major league clubs would lend a minor league team two or three ballplayers for the right to select any or all independent players off that minor league team's roster at the end of the season.

"That was a high price for what we got," John said. "We knew they were not going to send any of their top ballplayers, but marginal ones, at best. They did work cooperatively with us; they wouldn't send us an outfielder to play second base. On top of that, our clubs tried to sign the best local players they could find."

The period from 1948 to 1953 might have been the last time when local clubs had the initiative to go out and get the best young talent in the area and develop it. A good number of local ballplayers from the Western Carolina League towns went on to play in higher levels of Minor League Baseball, and some played in the major leagues. So the Western Carolina League was more than local entertainment; it was a real proving ground.

"We had a number of players from colleges in North Carolina," Moss said. "Belus Smawley came from Appalachian State to play in our league that summer. He was a heck of a basketball player too and was playing for the professional St. Louis Bombers at that time. The league had Don Stafford from Lenoir-Rhyne, a big, tall, home-run hitting first baseman who is now in the SAL Hall of Fame. There were two pitchers from Western Carolina College, Warren Deyermond, a master of the curveball, and fireballer Lawson Brown."

The WCL began play on May 1 and ended September 1. Lincolnton won the pennant and the playoffs, beating Morganton in the first round and Newton-Conover in the finals.

Shelby and Forest City disputed fourth place at the end of the season. Forest City was a few percentage points ahead of Shelby but had played two fewer games. The league's board of directors ordered Forest City to play a rained-out game with Shelby that had made a difference in the standings, but Shelby declined to play and Forest City went into the playoffs.

Hendersonville, with the largest ballpark, drew the fewest spectators, 35,768 for the season. Attendance for the other WCL clubs in that initial 1948 season ranged from 38,000 to more than 65,000 in Morganton.

"All in all," John said, "the season went well. We finished the year in good financial shape and didn't have any teams quit until Hendersonville dropped out at season's end."

The addition of the Western Carolina League put North Carolina over the top as having the greatest number of professional teams in

John Henry Moss and fellow members of the Western Carolina League take a ride on the Goodyear Blimp to get a bird's-eye view of the new minor league circuit's topography in 1948.

the nation in 1948. There were fifty-nine cities playing pro baseball in the Tar Heel state. Texas was second with fifty-eight. The nation had fifty-eight leagues that year, second highest ever, topped only by the fifty-nine leagues in 1949, involving 438 cities and towns.

With Major League Baseball confined to the northern and Midwestern states, and televised games still somewhere around the corner, folks in the remainder of the country flocked to see their minor league teams play.

Chapter 7
UMPIRING: BASEBALL'S TOUGHEST JOB

The quality of umpiring in the early Western Carolina League was not the caliber that exists in the minor leagues today. With 438 minor league clubs playing every night throughout the United States, the number of good umpires was stretched thin.

"We got as many umpires from umpiring schools as we could," John said, "and mixed them with capable local umpires. The locals were men who could have umpired steadily in the minors but didn't want to leave home and travel that much, so they were available and jumped at the chance to make extra money. All of our umpires were certified by the National Association, including the local fellows, most of whom had minor league or semipro experience in industrial leagues or who had umpired college games in the Southern Conference, which then included most of the Atlantic Coast Conference universities of today.

"A fellow named William Carpenter was supervisor of minor league umpires in the national office," John said. "He tried his best to keep things straight all over the country and did a good job too. He would try to help us find umpires when we needed them."

Geography contributed to economic factors in the WCL. All of the league's cities were so closely bunched that no one, neither players nor umpires, had to make overnight trips. Teams traveled back and forth to their games, spending nights in their own beds, and so did the umpires. This saved franchises thousands of dollars.

Despite the fact that many of his umpires were residents of the league's towns, Moss said he never heard the word "partiality" used. "We never had a 'homer'," he said, "and no one ever reported to me that they heard the expression used in the stands."

The reasons most of the local umpires Moss hired had quit umpiring previously were travel and low pay. "In other leagues where travel was necessary, they didn't want to be away from home that long," Moss said, "and a man could hardly support a family on minor league umpiring pay, especially living on the road through the summer. But in our league they could go to any town and umpire a night game and be back home usually by midnight. Many held daytime jobs. Johnny Shives did, and he sent two boys through Duke Medical School. He was one of the finest umpires I've ever had."

There were some interesting characters among the Western Carolina League umpires, like Baxter Moose, John Sherrill, Doc Kanupp, and John Price. They were interesting and capable but sometimes got too much of the spotlight. They were showmen who often created mirth in the league.

"I preached to them to stay in the background," John Henry said, "but I didn't punish them for not doing so. I remember one named Art Talley, who was a whale of a showman. He was umpiring a game in which Bob Bowman of the Morganton Aggies was pitching against Ray Lindsey of the Newton-Conover Twins. Bowman was a good-sized guy, about six foot one and 180 pounds, who later played the outfield and pitched a little for the Philadelphia Phillies for five seasons.

"Newton-Conover won the game in extra innings, and Bowman left the field mad about a decision Talley had made. After the game Bowman went to the cold drink machine for a Coke and encountered Talley, who had also gone to refresh himself.

"We didn't have all the antifraternization rules baseball later adopted," Moss said, "and they got to joshing each other about the call Talley had made. Bowman threatened to hit Talley with his Coke bottle, and Talley said he would hit him back. They went round and round, trying to crown each other with bottles until someone broke them apart. That's what the heat of the game can do to you. Here were two big, healthy men who didn't need Coke bottles to hit anybody."

Moss fined Talley and suspended him, and let Bowman off with a fine because he was the lesser of the two evils, so to speak.

"We had several good umpires," Moss said. "John Price was a good umpire, but he was no choirboy. He was tough. Had a brother named Charlie who was a United States Marshal.

"Don Peacock was another good umpire. He was from Denton,

North Carolina, the hometown of Max Lanier, who had pitched fourteen seasons in the majors, mostly for the Cardinals. Lanier later managed in the WCL.

"The National Association wanted young umpires and we found all we could. Frank Umont was one we brought to the Western Carolina League. He went on to umpire in the American League."

Different umpires call plays differently, according to how they see the plays. They all follow the rules, but at times idiosyncrasies crop up, and players and managers have to adjust to the umpire's whims. In baseball today, you can see this at work, especially in calling balls and strikes. Few umpires call the same strike zone. Some call higher strikes than others, who call wider strikes. Players have to adjust at the plate to cope with this. This occurs today, even in the major leagues.

Moss had an umpire in 1948, Earl H. Barter, whom he had brought in from Tenants Harbor, Maine. He dressed the old-fashioned way in black suit, white shirt, and black bow tie, and wore a big balloon chest protector. He was getting up in age and had umpired for Judge Manley Llewellyn of Asheville in the Tri-State League in 1947. Lew had called John Moss and said Barter was a good, very experienced umpire, neat and clean, who would always be on time and would carry out the functions of a good umpire.

"He's just getting a little old," Llewellyn said. As an afterthought he added, "He does have a tendency to keep the home crowd happy."

John hired Barter because the WCL needed experienced umpires to team with newcomers. Barter was calling balls and strikes one day in a game between Newton-Conover and Lincolnton. Chunk Rudisell of Lincolnton, a good hitter and fast on his feet, popped a pitch into the alley and raced all the way to third for a triple. Red Mincy, the Lincolnton manager who occupied the third-base coaching box when his team was at bat, called time and got Rudisell off the base and out of earshot of the third baseman.

Mincy said, "Listen to me, don't you try to steal home. Don't even think about it. Barter's back there. Now, here's what's gonna happen: They're gonna pitch out but you're gonna stay on this base till somebody hits the ball on the ground to the outfield. I'll let you go then because they can't throw you out, but you don't make no damn move till I say go. Don't you go because Barter'll call your tail out. Understood?"

"Gotcha," Chunk answered.

The Newton-Conover pitcher pitched out on the next pitch— and Chunk took off to steal home.

"Come back here," Mincy shouted, but Chunk was already sliding into the plate. Barter called him out.

"I thought he made it," Mincy said later. "I thought Barter blew the call in favor of the home team, so I didn't know whether to chew out Chunk or Barter."

The game went on for sixteen innings until a Lincolnton batter hit a triple. Chunk, up next, redeemed himself by laying down a perfect bunt on a suicide squeeze, and Lincolnton won the game.

Red Mincy never forgot that call by Barter. Mincy went on to manage Knoxville in the Tri-State League for a spell, managed a couple more places, and then quit baseball and came back to North Carolina. He took a job with the state, managing a truck-weighing station where the Catawba River flows into Charlotte, and for years he talked about "that damn Rudisell" and "that damn play!"

John Henry had his office upstairs over a street corner restaurant in downtown Kings Mountain, and before the 1948 season began, he had an umpire meeting there. Barter drove a spic-and-span black A-model Ford down from Maine in time to attend the meeting. He arrived on time with all his equipment and was ready to work.

He asked John where he could find a place to clean his car. "Go to the service station down the street," John said. "They'll clean it for you."

"No, that's not what I mean," Barter said. "I want to get all the tar and gunk I've collected from the road off the bottom of the car."

John said, "Well, go on down the street a little farther, and there's a place where you can do that." Barter carried two jacks in the A-model and used both to jack up the rear of the car. He stretched out on his back under the car and with a little brush removed all the bits of tar and grime collected there. Then he jacked up the front end and did the same there.

"That's how fussy and meticulous he was," John said.

The umpires met in John's office the next day. John spent the morning going over the rules and other business and ended the meeting before lunch.

Going down the stairs to the restaurant beneath the office, one of the umpires, a young fellow named Marvin Spitzer, from Long Island, New York, yelled back up, "Mr. Barter, I left my rules and regulations on the couch up there. Would you bring them down for me?" To Moss the umpire said, "I'm in a hurry. I've got to get going."

From the top of the stairs, Barter replied, "Young man, you have just as much time as I have, twenty-four hours a day."

Moss still laughs about that. "I had never heard that before," he said, "and I don't think I've heard it since."

Moss can remember having to fire only one umpire, a young man named Devoil Butcher, who had been an All-West Virginia high school football player. He came to the Western Carolina League's umpiring school at Newton-Conover in 1948 and was good enough to merit a job.

Butcher umpired into the 1960s and was in Spartanburg calling a Western Carolinas League game in 1963 when the Spartanburg third baseman, a fellow named Tony Solaita, created an incident. Solaita was outspoken on the field and that day was riding Butcher viciously. Considering himself to have as much speed as anyone in the league, he was a runner at third when a Spartanburger hit a short outfield fly, and after the catch Solaita came speeding home. The throw, however, beat him to the plate, and Butcher called him out.

Solaita jumped up and down and gave Butcher a lot of mouth, and without saying a word in return, Butcher balled his fist and socked Solaita in the mouth, stretching him out at the plate.

Bob Wellman, managing Spartanburg, ran to the plate and asked, "What the hell are you doing, Butch?"

Butcher glared at him and balled the fist again, shook it in Wellman's face, and said, "You want a little of this?" Realizing how serious the consequences would be, Wellman wisely turned around and went back to the coaching box.

John Moss suspended Butcher and never rehired him as an umpire.

"I was mayor of Kings Mountain at the time," John said, "and I knew Butcher was a good boy, so I offered him a job at the town's water plant, and he accepted. He went on to become a fine water plant operator. One morning, Butcher pulled out of the water plant in his car and a truck T-boned him and killed him instantly. I was proud of him. His mother had passed on by that time and Butch left all his money, beyond funeral expenses, to a little orphan girl."

One day, before he was suspended from baseball, Butcher came into John's office and said, "I need to go home."

"You're not leaving me, are you?" John asked.

"No, we've had a problem at home."

"Are you sure there's nothing I can help you with?"

"No," Butcher said, "I don't think there is. My mother just shot and killed my father." He went home and came back and continued to ump until he socked Solaita.

Max Lanier managed the Lexington Giants in the Western Carolinas League for three seasons. In 1963, he managed Bobby Bonds, father of Barry Bonds, who broke Hank Aaron's record of 755 lifetime home runs in 2007. Bobby was a sure-fire big league prospect, and Max Lanier helped guide him toward the major leagues.

Lanier had problems with Devoil Butcher. Several Latin American players on Lanier's ball club seemed to get in trouble with Butcher every time he called a Lexington game. Butcher was an educated man who had studied Spanish and learned to understand the language very well. Every time one of Lanier's Latinos called Butcher a black-hearted villain, or worse, in Spanish, Butcher threw him out of the game.

In one game, he threw out four of Lanier's Latinos, one at a time, and Max went crazy. Finally, Max appealed to John Moss, who was observing the game from the stands near the Lexington dugout, and Butcher threw Max out too.

"He's throwing out my best ballplayers," Max griped to Moss. "I don't know why."

"I'll have a talk with the boy, Max," John Moss said.

"He won't like it," Max returned.

Then, for a while, Butcher threw the Latinos out of several other games, and Max would telephone John and complain. Finally, the Lexington club figured out that Butcher understood Spanish, and the players stopped cursing the umpire in their native tongue.

Lanier called Moss later and complained that another umpire had thrown some of his players out, and said, "I don't know what I'm going to do. I'm just going to have to retire from managing; I can't stand my best players getting thrown out every night."

John said, "Aw, now, Max, it can't be that bad. I believe it'll get better in the latter part of the season."

"Well," Max replied, "I sure hope we get there soon."

But he continued to gripe. Finally, John asked, "Max, you'd like to get to the majors as a manager, wouldn't you?"

Max said he would, and John said, "Can I ask you something else, Max?"

"Yeah, yeah, go ahead."

"Do you know how many folks have gone on from this league to umpire in the majors?"

"No."

"Well, do you know how many have gone out of this league to manage at the major league level?"

"No, I don't."

"The score is 5–0," John said. "Five umpires and no managers."

John and Max didn't talk umpiring again until Max was out of baseball. "One night we were in St. Petersburg at the baseball meetings," John said, "and Max's son, Hal, who was managing Gastonia, and Tommy Helms and I went to the dog track. Max had a job working the twenty-dollar window at the track, and when we went up to make our first bet, Max said to me, 'I know what the score is. Five to nothing. How many?'"

Some of the umpiring incidents were hilarious and others defied imagination. One occurred at Rock Hill, South Carolina, in 1965 in a game between Rock Hill and Gastonia. The latter team had a catcher named Hidalgo who was an excellent receiver. Bob Moose, later an outstanding pitcher with Pittsburgh, was on the mound that day for Gastonia, and John Price was the umpire. A well-educated man, Price was meticulous in his calling and was highly respected in the game.

John Moss was sitting with Eddie Stanky and Bob Clements, the latter the farm director for the Pittsburgh Pirates, and saw this happen. Stanky and Clements apparently did not because they made no comment. Neither umpire on the field realized what had happened until it was too late to change a decision.

Rock Hill had a runner on first and Moose made a wild pitch. As the ball bounced to the wall behind the plate, the runner took off for second. Without chasing the first ball to the wall, Hidalgo, who had a great arm, held out his throwing hand to Price, who popped another ball in it, and Hidalgo threw the runner out going into second. "That's the only time I've seen two balls in play at once," Moss said, "and nobody argued."

In that day, minor league players could get away with much more than today, because many umpires then, like most players, were neophytes in the game.

George Wilson managed Statesville in the WCL in 1961, and in a Statesville game one of those zip-zip-zap plays occurred that defied description, but Wilson got away with it. The other team had a runner on first and the next batter hit safely to left center field. The left fielder scooped up the ball and overthrew third, trying to nail the runner coming from first. Wilson was standing in front of the Statesville dugout, and the ball bounced and landed underneath his arm. While the runner was already into third, the batter-runner was rounding first, and Wilson made a perfect throw to second and the baseman applied the tag. The umpire signaled the out, and no one questioned the play.

"I was watching the game," John Moss said, "and I didn't notice it happen. Obviously neither the umpires nor the other team noticed it either."

That was the same George Wilson who played for Denver before he became a manager. He was playing right field in an exhibition game in Denver against the Yankees and snow from the previous night remained on the shaded ground in right field. George made several snowballs and placed them around his position.

In the game a Yankee hitter slugged one over his head and George raced halfway back, grabbed one of the snowballs, and threw the Yankee out at second. Barney Deary, who later became supervisor for minor league umpires, was calling that game and failed to notice the switch. The play stood as called, perhaps the only time a major league player was thrown out with a snowball!

Once John Moss was out of town and his wife, Elaine, was at home where John maintained the league office. The telephone rang about five o'clock and someone from the Greenville club said, "One of the umpires is sick and can't work tonight. What should I do?"

"I'll get back to you," Elaine said, thinking fast.

She couldn't reach John by phone, so she contacted some American Legion baseball people in Kings Mountain and asked if they had the names of any umpires around Greenville. Luckily, she was given a name, and she telephoned the man in Greenville.

She told him who she was and what the problem was. "Can you help us out and call the bases there tonight?"

"I don't think I can," he replied. "I've got water on the knee."

Knowing no other solution to the problem, Elaine said, "I don't care about the water on your knee. Just put on a uniform and get to the ballpark as quickly as you can."

He did, and it worked out all right.

John said, "It's a great experience working with players and umpires who are just getting started in professional baseball. I think it's like a young lawyer fresh out of school going into a courtroom and the judge recognizing him right away as a beginner."

Danny Murtaugh managed the Pittsburgh Pirates to world championships in 1960 and 1971 and had done about everything in baseball—except umpire. One night in the 1970s he finally got his chance. He was visiting the Pittsburgh farm team in Gastonia to observe some of the Pirates' newly signed talent when suddenly John Henry Moss descended on him and asked him to umpire.

Doc Kanupp, who later became a member of the SAL Hall of

Fame, and his partner Bob Raines had umpired a series in Greenville and were driving to Gastonia to call the game there when their fan belt broke, marooning them on Interstate 85 until they could get help. They called ahead and advised the Gastonia team of their dilemma. Moss, who had come to Gastonia to see the game and to visit with Murtaugh, knew they couldn't get the fan belt repaired in time to reach the park for the start of the game. He did not want to delay the start and looked around for a solution.

He saw Murtaugh standing in the Gastonia dugout and snapped his fingers. "I'll get Danny to umpire," he said to himself. John thought Danny would be highly capable of umpiring because he had "umpired" for many years from the manager's seat on the bench in the Pittsburgh dugout.

Moss went to the dugout and said, "Danny, why don't you go out there and umpire till my umpires get here? They've had car trouble and can't make it on time. You won't have to call the whole game, but I'd like to get the game started on time."

"Yeah, yeah," Danny said. "I'll umpire. I can umpire."

"This is an official game," John said, "and you're being offered an opportunity to become an official professional baseball umpire."

"I'll do it. Give me a cap, son." A kid ran in the clubhouse and got Danny a cap. As he started to the field, he said to Moss, "I'm gonna umpire behind the pitcher. I ain't getting behind that batter."

"That's okay," John returned.

The game's first three innings passed uneventfully and the umpires still hadn't arrived, so Murtaugh, having a good time, continued to work. He was cramming baseballs into both hip pockets, and in the fourth inning a ball fell out of his right hip pocket. He stooped and retrieved the ball and put it back in his pocket. A pitch or two later a ball fell out of his left hip pocket. When he bent down to get that ball, his trousers split. Undaunted, he umpired through the fifth inning when Kanupp and Raines showed up and took over to start the sixth.

In his embarrassing condition, Murtaugh remained in the Gastonia dugout for the remainder of the game. He sent for Moss before the end of the sixth, and when John stepped into the dugout, he said, "Danny, I certainly appreciate your helping us out."

"Buddy," Danny said, "it's going to cost you some money. Look here." He turned and showed the rip in his trousers.

"I'll take care of it," John said, and promptly forgot it.

The following March, John encountered Murtaugh in spring training, and the Pittsburgh manager growled, "Wha'cha gonna do about my trousers?"

"Oh, I'm going to do something about them, Danny."

"When?"

"It won't be long."

But it was.

That went on for a couple of seasons, and John ran into him again in Pittsburgh. "Listen," Murtaugh gruffed his voice, "you oughta take care of that obligation you have on those trousers."

"Danny," Moss responded, "I'll do that."

So at Christmastime, John Moss and Dusty Gardner, president of the Gastonia club, telephoned Mrs. Murtaugh and got Danny's measurements. They had a pair of blue jeans tailored and sent them to him for Christmas.

John received a note in return that read, "Late, but nevertheless appreciated."

Murtaugh managed the Pirates through the 1976 season and died in early December. But he enjoyed his jeans until his death.

Who ever said umpiring wasn't fun?

Chapter 8
A NEW DIRECTION

John Henry Moss was president of the Western Carolina League the first time for that one season only, 1948. He thought his rookie season as a professional league president had been a success, probably helped along by the fact that some of the players in the league were older than he was.

At the end of the season, the league's directors made no attempt to renew John's one-year contract. "They didn't fire me," he said, "but just took their time about rehiring me. I think they wanted to wait till the end of October at the annual meetings, which would have been all right, but I would have signed a new contract any time after the season ended."

In the meantime, the Class B Tri-State League club in Rock Hill, South Carolina, knowing of John's solid work with the WCL, came calling and offered him the general manager's job. "That," he said, "was an opportunity for me to jump from Class D to Class B, which today would be the equivalent of going from Class A to AA. I accepted the Rock Hill job with a considerable increase in salary."

The Western Carolina League hired Cloyd A. Hager of Hickory to replace Moss as president for the 1949 season. Hager left after two years, and P. W. Deaton and T. Earl Franklin held the position for a year each before the league closed its doors and folded after the 1952 season, victim of too much overpayment of players' salaries. Simply, the league went broke because it violated salary limits.

The original eight WCL teams of 1948 made up the league in 1949. The only change was the name of the Forest City Owls. They became the Spindale Owls, operated by the same Rutherford County Amusement Company and used the same stadium the Forest City Owls had occupied the previous season. Forest City and Spindale were twin Rutherford County towns of the same size who shared the team.

Under Moss's general managership, Rock Hill finished fourth in the eight-team Tri-State League in 1949, behind pennant-winning Florence, South Carolina, Spartanburg, and Asheville. The Rock Hill Chiefs also had the league's third highest attendance, 98,237, behind Spartanburg's 128,490 and Asheville's 105,899.

Two outstanding moves that Moss made that season were to acquire the contracts of outfielder James Lamar (Dusty) Rhodes and Jim Pearce. Rhodes later became an excellent pinch-hitter for the New York Giants. Pearce jumped all the way from Rock Hill to the major leagues at the end of the Tri-State League season. Even though he pitched five partial seasons for the Washington Senators and Cincinnati Reds, his record in the majors was undistinguished.

The Chicago Cubs had given up on Dusty Rhodes as a prospective major league outfielder, and the Senators had also dropped Pearce from their planning for the future. "I acquired both of their contracts and signed them," Moss said. "I signed several other veteran ballplayers, especially pitchers, because we knew the Giants would load up Knoxville and Mr. Rickey and the Brooklyn Dodgers would load up Asheville, which had won the Tri-State League pennant for Mr. Rickey by seventeen and a half games in 1948."

Moss hired such ballplayers as Tommy Kerr, a right-handed pitcher, and thirty-eight-year-old Johnny Lanning of Asheville, who had pitched eleven seasons in the majors for the Boston Braves and Pittsburgh Pirates. He also signed two other ex-major leaguers in Wally Chipple, who had played briefly for Washington, and Eddie Freed, a veteran of the Philadelphia Phillies.

One day, Red Dwyer, owner of the Rock Hill club, told Moss that he knew of two pitchers who might help the team. "Can we afford them?" Dwyer asked.

"We can afford anybody you want to," Moss told Dwyer, whose money would pay most of their salaries. So John signed Ed Kibuski and Barney Schultz. He obtained Kibuski from the Trenton, New Jersey, club of the Class B Inter-State League, and signed Schultz as a free agent. Schultz pitched his way from Rock Hill to the big leagues and was a sound reliever for the St. Louis Cardinals, Detroit Tigers, and Chicago Cubs for seven seasons.

A year or two before that, Kibuski had had one of those hilarious experiences baseball players sometimes encounter. Pitching for Charlotte in the Tri-State League in 1947, Kibuski hung a curveball to Roy Smalley, the Fayetteville, North Carolina, shortstop, who hit the ball over the fence and deep into a cemetery to win the game. The disgusted Kibuski trudged back to the Charlotte dugout and sat languidly on the bench. Charlotte's manager, fiery Spencer Abbott, dumped a bucket of water on his head. Abbott then turned and walked away without saying a word.

Two years later, when John Moss signed Kibuski to pitch for Rock Hill, he asked the pitcher about the incident. "I was so shocked I never said anything about it to him, and he never said anything to me," Kibuski said.

In talent, John had a good ball club in Rock Hill. The Chiefs had the league's leading hitter in Bob Churchill, .360, and the league's lowest earned run average pitcher in Suvern Wright, 1.86.

"Wright could really throw the ball," Moss said. "He had pitched Spartanburg to the Junior American Legion World Series championship that spring, and after our season was over at Rock Hill he went up to Richmond in Triple-A.

"He had come to us from the Richmond club, which let us have him because he refused to report to Richmond. He was just a kid and I suppose the thought of going from Legion baseball into Triple-A must have overpowered him. We paid Richmond something like $500 to release him, with the stipulation that Richmond could claim him at the end of our season. We signed him and after playing that season near home, he went ahead and reported to Richmond."

The pitching staff kept Rock Hill in the race for the Tri-State League championship until late in the season. One of the Rock Hill pitchers, Bill Bustle, could spot his pitches as well as major leaguers. He was a sharp guy too. He pitched a couple of years in higher baseball and then went to Charleston, South Carolina, and was baseball coach at Charleston College.

Dusty Rhodes came to Rock Hill as a twenty-two-year-old outfielder who stood six feet tall and weighed 178 pounds. He threw right-handed and batted left-handed. He went on to the big leagues and played seven seasons with the New York Giants. His final year, in 1959, was the Giants' second season in San Francisco.

Rhodes was a deluxe pinch-hitter. Primarily because he was not a regular position player, his overall major league record wasn't overpowering. In 576 big league games, he batted .253, with 296 hits and 54 home runs. He also scored 146 times and knocked in 207 runners. Not exactly spectacular.

But the 1954 World Series was his moment of glory. He slugged the Giants to a four-game sweep of the favored Cleveland Indians and made baseball history. The Indians had that fabled pitching staff of Early Wynn (23–11), Bob Lemon (23–7), Mike Garcia (19–8), Bob Feller (13–3), and Art Houtteman (13–7).

Rhodes went into that series with good figures for the season. He had batted .341, with fifteen home runs for a slugging percentage of .695, and had knocked in fifty runs. He batted six times in the World Series and hit safely four times. As a pinch-hitter he went 3-for-3, and in the two games he played in the outfield, he was 1-for-3. He hit home runs in the first two games.

That was the World Series that produced the most amazing catch anyone could remember up to that time: Willie Mays' over-the-head, back-to-the-plate, running catch of Vic Wertz's 440-foot fly in the spacious Polo Grounds with two men on. The catch sent the game into the tenth inning, and Rhodes ended it, 5–2, with a three-run homer.

In the second game, Rhodes produced a pinch-hit single in the fifth to tie the game and homered in the seventh for an insurance run. The Giants won the game, 3–1.

Rhodes delivered a two-run pinch single in the third game to give the Giants a 3–0 lead. They won the game, 6–2.

Rhodes was the only Giant to homer in the series.

"At Rock Hill, we had enough pitching to stay with the other clubs that year," John said. "That's what kept us in the race until late in the season. Florence won the pennant, and Asheville had a good ball club. Frank Genovese, the Knoxville manager, had a guy who could hit the ball all the way to Chattanooga. It was an exciting season."

The most interesting extracurricular thing Moss promoted that 1949 season was a Celebrity Night in July. He invited celebrities from baseball, football, golf, tennis, basketball, and all sports played in North and South Carolina. (Well, almost all sports; Asheville had a polo team that summer from which no one was asked.) Pitcher Ernie Shore; Frank Packard, a great minor league home run hitter; Babe Dedrickson Zaharias, possibly the country's all-time best female athlete; Clemson basketball coach Banks McFadden and several players from the University of South Carolina and Clemson College; and others like Gene Blue, who pitched minor league ball many years before, were honored that evening.

One of the highlights of John Moss's career was when two of baseball's all-time greatest players attended that Celebrity Night: Cy Young, the all-time winningest major league pitcher with 511 victories—a record that can never be broken under baseball's present structure; and Shoeless Joe Jackson, baseball's third all-time leading hitter, who was banned from baseball for life after the Black Sox Scandal of 1919.

Cy Young, an eighty-two-year-old man at the time, had pitched twenty-two years in the majors, winning 509 regular season games and two games for the Boston Red Sox in the first World Series ever played, in 1903, when the Red Sox won the last two games to beat the Pittsburgh Pirates, five games to three. In his last victory in the seventh game, Young was aided by an archaic rule that permitted balls hit into the crowd sitting and standing around the outfield to go for triples; his teammates collected five triples on the rule that day.

Shoeless Joe, a South Carolinian born in Brandon Mills, had a lifetime batting average of .356, third all-time behind Ty Cobb's .367 and Rogers Hornsby's .358. Jackson played for the Philadelphia Athletics, Cleveland Indians, and Chicago White Sox. Even though he was the White Sox' leading hitter in the 1919 World Series with a .375 average, Jackson, an outfielder, along with pitchers Eddie Cicotte, Swede Risburg, and Claude (Lefty) Williams, first baseman Chick Gandil, outfielder Oscar (Happy) Felsch, third baseman Fred McMullin, and infielder Buck Weaver, were barred from Organized Baseball for life after the 1920 season for their part in what turned out to be a fixed series in 1919, which the White Sox lost to the Cincinnati Reds, five games to three.

To this day John Moss regrets one thing about his Celebrity

Night. He took Young and Shoeless Joe to one of the area's finest steak houses for dinner and relished the stories the two old-timers told, but he failed to have his picture made with them. "I regret that," he said. "Imagine what it would mean to have a picture today of yourself with those two! Sometime later, I went to the *Rock Hill Herald* to see if they had taken a photo of us, and they had, but they couldn't find it."

"Funny thing about that dinner," Moss added, "was that I purposely took them to a great steak house so they could be well fed. When we got there Shoeless Joe ate only dry toast and coffee, and Mr. Young ate mixed fruit and milk. So I had a steak. I was a young guy and I'd been running all day. I probably could have eaten two.

"But that Celebrity Night was one of the oddest and most pleasing experiences of my career in baseball—and one of the best promotions I ever pulled off." Baseball teams would do well to host similar promotions today.

Everywhere in baseball, amusing events occur. Moss recalls one from that season in Rock Hill when a tall umpire named Henry Winston accused Rock Hill manager Dick Bouknight of spitting on him during a rhubarb. Manley Llewellyn, president of the Tri-State League, suspended Bouknight for five games and fined him $75.

Moss thought the penalties were too strong but knew no one could do anything about the suspension. However, there was a way to have a little fun and get Bouknight's fine paid for him. Moss had someone pass a spittoon among the fans to collect Bouknight's fine, and folks put $125 in the cuspidor.

Moss has always suspected Furman Bisher, then sports editor of the *Charlotte News,* and for many years now, one of the best sports columnists in the country for the *Atlanta Journal-Constitution,* of tipping Llewellyn off, probably thinking it might create such a funny incident he could get a column out of it. Llewellyn telegraphed Moss, "I hereby direct you to give the fans' money to Red Cross charities," and John said he followed instructions.

When the Hot Stove League cranked up a half-century ago, talk always turned to long home runs, the kind of distance blows hit by

Mickey Mantle and Harmon Killebrew. But long home runs were not the sole property of the major leagues. There have been sluggers in the minors who could hit the ball out of sight.

"The longest home run I ever saw," John Moss said, "was hit by a young fellow from Statesville, North Carolina, in Sims Park in Gastonia one Sunday afternoon. I don't remember his name, but he hit the ball over the centerfield fence, and that was a long, long way in that ballpark. I would say he hit that ball over five hundred feet.

"There was a boy who played in the Western Carolina League," Moss said, "who hit long home runs with regularity. His name was Bob Robertson. The Pittsburgh Pirates had signed him and sent him to Gastonia, the Pittsburgh farm team. Gastonia finished third, three games out, in 1965, and Robertson hit thirty-two home runs and knocked in ninety-eight runs to lead the league. He had great competition that season: Bobby Bonds scored a league-leading 103 runs for Lexington; and Al (Scoop)Oliver, Robertson's teammate at

John Henry Moss is in some impressive company at the Hot Stove banquet in January 2008 in Raleigh, North Carolina. Pictured from left to right are Carolina League President John Hopkins, John Henry Moss, National Association President Pat O'Conner, Senior Manager of Minor League Operations for Major League Baseball Sylvia Lind, and South Atlantic League President Eric Krupa.

Gastonia, had 159 hits to lead the league. All three of those fellows had long major league careers.

"That was a year we had some pretty good managers in the Western Carolina League. Chuck Churn managed Salisbury to the pennant for the Houston Astros. Clyde Sukeforth managed at Gastonia, Max Lanier at Lexington, Wes Ferrell at Shelby, and Sparky Anderson at Rock Hill."

Bob Robertson moved on up to Asheville in the Class AA Southern League in 1966 and led the league with thirty-two home runs and ninety-nine runs batted in. He hit exceptionally long home runs in the thin mountain air of Asheville's McCormick Field that summer. About ten feet behind the leftfield fence in Asheville, behind the 375-foot mark, stood a wooden light pole roughly ninety feet high. Robertson cleared that light four times that summer. No one could recall anyone else ever hitting a ball over the pole.

"Home run hitting is strange," Moss said. "A lot of people hit home runs, but only a few hit really long home runs."

Perhaps the longest home run not on record was hit by a Cuban outfielder named Bobby Estalella, who led the Class B Piedmont League with thirty-three home runs for Charlotte in 1937. The story was told that Estalella hit one home run all the way to Gastonia. Old Hyman Park in Charlotte was built beside the railroad yards that lay just beyond the centerfield fence. Estalella cleared the fence one day and the ball went in the open door of a moving boxcar that didn't stop until the train reached Gastonia.

"That sounds like Jake Wade to me," John Moss laughed. Wade was sports editor of the *Charlotte Observer* in those days and widely known for the tall tales he told.

Chapter 9
CLIMBING THE LADDER

Opportunity knocked at the Moss door in the fall of 1949. John was sitting in his office while two high school football teams played a game in the baseball park. Zip Hannah, Rock Hill's chief of police, who had played football for the University of South Carolina and the Washington Redskins, stepped to the door and said, "Come out here, John; I want you to see something."

They sat in the bleachers watching Columbia High School play Friendship High of Rock Hill.

"Watch this guy run," Hannah said when Columbia took over the ball. Suddenly, a halfback broke loose and ran the ball for a dazzling sixty-yard touchdown. It was an impressive run, zigging in and zagging out, and John asked, "Who is that fellow?"

"His name is J. C. Caroline," Hannah said. "You'll hear a lot about him before long." Indeed, the entire nation did. J. C. Caroline became one of the premier runners in the United States at the University of Illinois and had an illustrious career with the Chicago Bears in the National Football League.

Little did Moss know that he was within minutes of receiving a telephone call that would take him to a better baseball job and also an opportunity to work in professional football.

The telephone rang and John went in to answer it. "John, this is Ray Kennedy of the Detroit Tigers." Kennedy had managed Asheville to the 1928 SAL pennant by an eighteen-game margin.

"What can I do for you, Mr. Kennedy?"

"We would like to talk to you about joining the Detroit Tigers' farm system." Word always gets around when someone does a good job in baseball, either on the field or in the office.

"Well, I certainly would be interested," Moss said.

"Can you come to Detroit Tuesday?" Kennedy asked. "Fly up and we'll cover the costs."

"Yes, I'll be there."

Before John made the trip to Detroit, Rube Wilson, a veteran of many baseball campaigns, offered some advice. John always thought Rube was one of the best minor league managers and a man who knew baseball. "Take the job, John," Rube advised. "Be your own boss, then you won't have to answer to all these people."

When John boarded the plane for Detroit in Charlotte the next week, he found himself seated beside Bob Feller, the great Cleveland Indians fireball pitcher who was on his way to Cleveland to negotiate his contract for 1950. Feller led the American League in number of pitching victories six times.

"I never enjoyed an airplane ride more," John said. "Bob Feller and I have been good friends all the years to this day."

John took the job with Detroit and stayed with the Tigers five years, 1950 through 1954, in a portion of his career that he calls "truly enjoyable."

The Tigers sent him to Jamestown, New York, as general manager of their club in the Class D PONY League (the Pennsylvania-Ohio-New York League). He was there for the 1950 season only and then worked as general manager of Detroit's clubs in Richmond, Indiana, in the Ohio-Indiana League, and Wausau in the Wisconsin State League. In Wausau he branched out into other areas. He became general manager of the Wausau professional football team

John Henry Moss (far left) reviews the roster while welcoming players of the Jamestown (New York) Falcons in 1950. Moss is pictured alongside Bob Shawkey, who pitched the first game at Yankee Stadium when it opened in 1923. Shawkey was the Falcons' manager when Moss served as general manager of the club.

in the Central States League; he established a booking agency called
John Moss and Associates; and after that became vice president
of the International Safety Company, which marketed all sorts of
safety devices for various things, including burglar alarm systems
for homes.

Bob Shawkey was Jamestown's field manager in 1950. He was a
great pitcher and four-time twenty-game winner for the Yankees in
the 1910s and 1920s. Detroit liked him to instruct their best young
pitchers.

The Jamestown newspaper greeted new Falcons business manager John
Henry Moss to town with an honorary cartoon.

John McHale, the Tigers' general manager, called John from Detroit one day and said, "We just signed a boy out of the University of Alabama, name of Frank Lary. He can throw, John. He's twenty years old and is a sure major leaguer. We're sending him to you, so pick him up this afternoon at the airport in Westfield."

Moss told Shawkey that he was going to Westfield to pick up a new pitcher and told him what McHale had said about the young man. "Hmm," Shawkey mused. "We're playing a doubleheader tonight and, if you get him back in time, I'll start him in the second game. It's a seven-inning game, and I can get him out of there if I have to. We'll see what he has."

Lary was a nice young man, John said. He met Lary at the airport and, as they drove back toward Jamestown, they passed Lake Chautauqua. There were a lot of roadside stands around the lake, from which farmers sold home-grown fruit, and several had some good-looking grapes.

Frank saw the grapes as they went by, and said, "I haven't had anything to eat since breakfast."

John said, "Well, Bob Shawkey said he wants you to start the second game."

"The hell you say!" Lary exclaimed. "Stop! Stop! Let's get a bag of those grapes. I've got to have something to eat before I pitch."

Lary ate grapes the remainder of the way to Jamestown, suited up quickly at the ballpark, and went out to pitch the second game. "He pitched a one-hitter," John said, "and got two hits himself. That was Frank Lary's professional beginning. You will remember that he became a Yankee-killer for the Tigers in the 1950s and 1960s."

Jamestown finished in sixth place that season, but drew 60,790 fans, third best in the eight-team league and only 7,000 fewer than the attendance at pennant-winning Hornell, New York.

Those were learning years for John Moss, and while he learned, he oversaw the operation of four different Detroit farm clubs. At the end of that 1950 season in Jamestown, John was sent to Buffalo, New York, as assistant general manager of the AAA International League team there. The Bisons were struggling. They finished the season in last place, thirty-seven games behind the Rochester Royals, who won the league pennant.

When Moss finished that season he was transferred to Richmond, Indiana, where the Detroit farm club finished third in 1951 in the Class D Ohio-Indiana League, thirty-seven and a half games off the pace. That league was troubled that year, as were many others in the minors. The circuit had dropped to five teams, and Newark fell out in July, reducing the field to four.

John was moved by Detroit to Wausau, Wisconsin, in the Class D Wisconsin State League for the 1952 season. Manager Mike Tresh brought the team home in second place, drawing about 40,000 fans. Moss remained in Wausau another season, finishing second again in 1953; the Wisconsin State League folded after that season.

John remained in Wausau as general manager of the Wausau professional football team and worked in his recently organized firm of John Moss and Associates in the entertainment promotional business.

Chapter 10
FRINGE BENEFITS

Wausau's pro football team, the Wausau Muskies, played in the Central States Professional Football League, which covered Minnesota, Michigan, Illinois, and Wisconsin. The league had franchises in Minneapolis, Minnesota; Grand Rapids, Michigan; Waukegan, Illinois; and Delevan, Wausau, and Racine, Wisconsin.

As general manager of the Wausau football team, he immediately found that directing a pro football team was different than the general manager's duties in minor league baseball. "The biggest change I found," John said, "was in the age of the players. In baseball we were dealing with kids who were just breaking into the professional game, most of them fresh out of high school, but I found that in football the players were older and more responsible.

"In Wausau, we signed former players from the University of Wisconsin and a couple more nearby schools. We also signed several who had been cut by the Green Bay Packers and Chicago Cardinals of the National Football League."

The two leagues, the NFL and the Central States League, were in no way connected. This was not called a minor league, but simply a league.

The Wausau Muskies' roster included lawyers, salesmen, teachers, and men from various other fields. Three of the team members had been All-Americans at Wisconsin and another at the University of Iowa, and all could still play the game.

"All the players," John said, "were already focused on their careers outside football. They were on a reality level that was more in tune with mine than young baseball players. Directing them was mostly a matter of meeting their needs. We paid them well for their football play on weekends and practice time through the week."

Over the three seasons John ran the front office, George Paskvan coached the team through the first two seasons, followed by Red

Voight, and both were good coaches who were so in tune with the players' needs that Wausau won the league championship all three years. An assistant coach was Bob Hanslic, who had played with the Philadelphia Eagles and was a Wisconsin classmate of Elroy (Crazy Legs) Hirsch, a great pass-catching end for the Los Angeles Rams at that time. Hirsch is enshrined in the Pro Football Hall of Fame. Because they had only five league opponents, the Muskies scheduled games with other teams, like Fort Leonard Wood, the St. Louis Knights, Detroit Stars, and Chicago Ravens.

John ran into some strange and humorous situations in football, the same as he encountered at times in baseball. One season he signed a fellow named Ronnie Ashe, who played tackle and also loved to strum his guitar. On road trips, each player was responsible for carrying his own gear. Helmets were shipped air freight in boxes, but the players carried their shoulder pads, jerseys, and pants in hanger bags.

"That saved us the trouble and expense of having to box all that stuff and ship it by air," John said. The team flew to road games.

For one game, Ashe could not carry all his equipment and his guitar too, so he left his shoulder pads at home and took his guitar along. The one thing a football player needs more than anything else is shoulder pads, and Ashe wound up at the airport without his.

"No way you can wear that guitar," Coach Paskvan told him when he discovered Ashe's choice of personal cargo, "and we can't wait for you. We have to take off right away, so get on in and maybe we'll find something."

"Ashe got on the plane," John said, "and all the players clamored for him to play his guitar, which he did. He was good. I thought it was funny and also strange that here was a young man getting paid to play football who had brought his guitar along but left his shoulder pads at home." John scouted around and finally borrowed a set of shoulder pads from the opposing team, but they were so small for Ashe that he hardly made a dent in the game.

John Henry knew that for him football was only a stopgap in his pursuit of a baseball career, but it was an opportunity to make some off-season money. He launched himself into football with the same zest with which he worked in baseball, but he knew all along that his future lay on the diamond. However, he was also making strides in the business world.

In 1955, John organized John Moss and Associates, a combination promotions agency, booking agency, and public relations firm, and with it launched himself into the world of entertainment promotions. Actually, this was not far removed from his career of being a general manager of baseball teams, because the latter job delved hugely in promotions to lure fans into baseball parks. He attended most of his promotions in person and was always delighted to see the talent he brought to various towns score successes.

Working primarily in Wisconsin, Minnesota, Iowa, and Michigan, Moss booked stars like Johnny Cash and other top-notch country and western talent for concert tours. "There were a lot of ballrooms in that area," John said, "and we promoted big bands in many of them. That was a good business." He also booked championship rodeos in the Midwestern states, but on occasion he ranged outside that area and booked rodeos as far away as Atlanta.

John had his first encounter with politics through his promotions firm and wound up raising funds for both the Democrat and Republican parties.

Walter Kohler was the Republican governor of Wisconsin, and John agreed to raise funds for the party. Bob Dean, attorney for the Wausau football team, and who rose to the position of federal judge, knew that John had taken on the task of raising funds for the Republicans, so he approached John with a similar request.

"I am chairman of the Democrat party in Marathon County," he said. "I need someone to raise funds for us. I've been busy handling your taxes for two years and keeping you out of trouble with the tax people." Put that way, there was no way John could refuse the request, so he agreed and found himself in the unusual situation of raising funds for both parties.

One evening Dean asked John, "Are you going to be in town this weekend?"

"I think so," John said.

"I'll call you tomorrow," the lawyer said, "and we may want to get together about raising money."

The next day Dean telephoned again and said, "We're going

down to Madison tomorrow and meet with these people so you can tell us how to raise funds."

"Okay," John said. "What time do we have to be down there, about twelve o'clock?" It was about one hundred and fifty miles to Madison.

"No," Dean said. "Nine o'clock. We have to be there at nine o'clock."

"I got up in the middle of the night," John said, "and we left about six o'clock. We made the two-and-a-half-hour drive with a few minutes to spare.

"I came up with the card method of fund-raising, so much for card-carrying members—five dollars, or ten—and then showed them how to organize it.

"It was easy for them to organize because Wisconsin, being mostly flat, is laid out in blocks. Property owners had once identified their land by using oak or sycamore trees or large boulders for corner boundaries. But when we were planning, those oaks and sycamores weren't there any more and it would have taken counties a hundred years to sort out the ownership of all property, so I set up a more simple system, which worked for them. They were successful in raising needed funds. Pat Lucy, who went on to become lieutenant governor and then governor of Wisconsin, was part of that fund-raising group."

John Henry worked as a promoter for two and a half years and then closed the doors of his agency and joined the International Safety Company of Minneapolis in the early part of 1957. He remained with that firm for two and a half years, eventually rising to the office of vice president, and became the company's representative in the Southeastern states.

One day at the baseball park in 1957, John Henry met a young lady named Elaine Beilke who changed his life. "She attended many of our games," John said. "I asked her for a date one evening, and we began dating rather regularly. She was controller of supplies for a national manufacturer, and that fall, after we had been dating a while, she became publicity director for the Wausau football team." That threw the two closer together and their courtship grew.

Matrimonial obsessions entered the romance. Before the year was out, on December 27, 1957, John and Elaine were married. John continued to work with the International Safety Company. With an eye to expanding operations to the southern states, the company assigned John to head the southern operations. On March 15, 1959, he returned to Kings Mountain, bringing his bride with him.

"I came home with all expectations of remaining in the business I was in," John said, "but on Palm Sunday of 1959, my old buddies from the Western Carolina League came calling and asked me to reorganize the Western Carolina baseball league."

At first, John was reluctant to give up his good job with the International Safety Company. "Boys," he told his visitors, "I promised my wife I was going to stick to business."

They argued back and forth and John began to feel the tug of excitement that baseball has always generated in him.

"Tell you what," he said, hedging a bit, "I'll let you know."

Chapter 11
A CALL TOO GREAT

The call of baseball was too great for John Henry Moss to resist, and on June 29, 1959, five years after he left the Detroit organization and the game of baseball, John and his friends met at the Elks Club in Gastonia and reorganized the Western Carolina League, which had been idle since the 1952 season. John was elected president of the league.

For the next fifty years, he served as the league's president—through thick and thin, through much expansion of its boundaries up and down the Eastern seaboard, and through a change of name to the South Atlantic League (the oldest and most revered minor league in the nation dating from 1904). John loved every minute of the work. The present league stands as a monument to the time and effort he spent building it.

"I don't think I would have been happy staying out of baseball," John said, "and both Elaine and I knew it. She was a young married woman who was going to go along with whatever her husband wanted to do—and I wanted to be in baseball. We laughed about that many times afterward."

At that meeting in Gastonia, John and his friends felt they were resurrecting a horse most of baseball thought dead but that still had life in it. The league was reorganized by John and some of his former owners in the original WCL and some new friends who were interested in investing. The cities accepted for league membership were Lexington, Salisbury, Hickory, Shelby, Statesville, and Gastonia, plus Newton and Conover as one team and Rutherford County as another. All had been members of the WCL previously, and all were in North Carolina.

It was from this point that the industriousness, the truly great leadership, and knowledge of the game really began to show in John Henry Moss. This was the last time he changed jobs.

Permit us to set the stage here for the task that lay ahead for John Moss. He knew he was challenged by a nearly impossible task in making the Western Carolina League a success in the face of the greatest decline the minor leagues had ever experienced. When many failing minors viewed the expansion of the majors as something like encroachment, John looked upon it as something inevitably destined to occur, and he began to search for ways to capitalize on this surge of the majors.

Consider first that the whole structure of baseball changed during the decade of the 1950s after John had left the game, not just in the minor leagues but in the majors as well. To the delight of fans across America, television was responsible for much of the change, and major league games suddenly came into their living rooms on television. Remember those great telecasts of the World Series in the early 1950s during that fabulous five-year bombardment by the Yankees as World Series champions from 1949 through 1953? Remember how Americans crowded around television sets to watch them? Regular season games soon became available on television across the country on Saturdays.

Television changed more than baseball. It changed the whole country. Folks could watch the Yankees play the St. Louis Browns on Saturday afternoon and Milton Berle that night. Lord have mercy! What would they think of next? Actually a thousand things were thought of next. Hog-calling contests, lumberjack tournaments, rodeos, all in your living room. All of these things took people away from local minor league baseball parks.

The minor leagues went into a nosedive in the 1950s. As the decade began, Organized Baseball contained fifty-eight minor leagues, most of them thriving. But as the nation moved from the fifties into the 1960s, there were only twenty-two minor leagues remaining. The cause of this demise of thirty-six leagues was surely dwindling attendance that put many teams and whole leagues into red ink.

Major League Baseball realized that many other American cities had grown to big-league size, and they began to switch franchises from city to city, spreading big league baseball from their previous confines of the Northeast and Midwest to the West Coast, Texas, the Deep South, and even beyond the nation's borders into Canada. At the start of the 1950s, both the National and American leagues contained eight teams, just as they had for half a century. The time line that follows illustrates the speed with which changes and expansion occurred, beginning in the 1950s and continuing through the present time:

1953 – The Boston Braves made the first move, switching their National League franchise to Milwaukee for the season.

1954 – The St. Louis Browns, who had gained the reputation of a loveable doormat for the American League – the same as the early New York Mets would be for the National League in future years – switched locations to Baltimore.

1955 – The Philadelphia Athletics moved westward to Kansas City.

1958 – The big move came for the 1958 season when the Dodgers transferred to Los Angeles and the Giants to San Francisco, leaving baseball's largest market – New York City – entirely in the hands of the Yankees. The Dodgers played in the mammoth Los Angeles Coliseum, which had been built for the 1932 Olympic Games and then used for football. Fitting a baseball field in the Coliseum required some modifications, which were made at the loss of a few hundred seats. Neither the Dodgers nor the Giants had any trouble fitting into their new communities, but had they needed any assistance, the Dodgers brought it when they won the 1959 World Series over the Chicago White Sox.

1961 – The American League expanded into California with the birth of the Los Angeles Angels, which later became the California Angels and still later the Anaheim Angels. The club was founded and owned by Gene Autry, the singing cowboy star of the silver screen in the 1930s and 1940s. Also a new Washington Senators team was put in the nation's capital to replace the Senators, who had moved to the Twin Cities of Minneapolis and St. Paul and changed their name to thes Minnesota Twins.

1962 – The National League opened the season with a new team in New York, the Metropolitans, called Mets for short, and a new team, the Colt .45s, in Houston. The latter nickname was changed to the Astros in 1965, in honor of NASA's space flight center in Houston.

1966 – The Braves, who had moved from Boston to Milwaukee thirteen years before, moved again to Atlanta, where they would become the winningest franchise in baseball during the decade of the 1990s.

1968 – The Kansas City Athletics, under the ownership of Charlie Finley, a controversial innovator of baseball, switched to Oakland, California, where Finley changed the face of the game by dressing his team in green, gold, and white uniforms and white shoes, a softball-like appearance theretofore unheard of in the staid old gray-and-white game.

1969 – The American League moved into Seattle with the establishment of a franchise known as the Seattle Pilots, and a new club named the Royals was placed in Kansas City. That same year, Montreal with its Expos and San Diego with the Padres entered the National League, the latter giving baseball six teams on the Pacific Coast.

1970 – After only a year playing in an open stadium in the rainy confines of Seattle, the Pilots moved to Milwaukee and became the Brewers, named so because Milwaukee was known for its major industry. Remember Schlitz – the beer that made Milwaukee famous?

1971 – The Washington Senators moved again, this time to the Dallas-Fort Worth area of Texas to begin play in 1972 as the Texas Rangers. This franchise was later owned by George W. Bush, who became President of the United States in 2001.

1977 – The American League opened up in Canada with the Toronto Blue Jays, and another American League team was established in Seattle, the Mariners.

1993 – After more than a decade with relatively little change, Denver, Colorado, and Miami, Florida, were accepted as expansion teams by the National League, the Denver team known as the Rockies and the Miami team dubbed the Florida Marlins.

1995 – Franchises were established by the American League in Tampa Bay, Florida, named the Devil Rays, and in the National League in Phoenix, Arizona, called the Arizona Diamondbacks. Neither of these teams began to play until the 1998 season, giving them time to create organizations and line up players.

1996 – Milwaukee switched from American League membership to the National League.

If all of this is somewhat confusing, so it was for baseball fans who tried valiantly to keep up with the game's changing face.

There was a downside to all this expansion. All of these franchise changes in the majors, spreading the game across the land, forced minor league teams to fall like flies.

Thus, the face of Major League Baseball had already changed

Baseball Commissioner Peter Ueberroth and John Henry Moss pose for a photo opportunity at the Winter Meetings in the mid-1980s. Over Moss's left shoulder is National Association President Johnny Johnson.

when John Henry Moss twice went before the big league farm directors in December of 1959 to ask for player support and financial assistance for the fledgling WCL and was turned down on both occasions. Moss had told the farm directors when they turned him down the second time that the Western Carolina League would play with or without their assistance—and this was before affiliation with the Continental League occurred to him. Some may have thought that to be a rash statement, but that was before they came to know John Henry Moss.

Chapter 12
THE PRICE GOES UP

Money has changed baseball more than anything else. At one time, boys grew toward manhood thinking they would like to become president of the United States, but that is lost in the past. Now they want to play right field for the New York Yankees or pitch for the Atlanta Braves.

Once, the lesser-paid baseball players in the major leagues often barely made enough money to live. As far as is known, no one ever starved playing baseball, but it used to be that folks, even some players, wondered how they were going to make ends meet. Baseball was not the greatest paying trade in the world until one became an established player—then he made good money.

Today, when people think of the astronomical, multimillion-dollar payrolls of Major League Baseball, they can lose perspective in relation to their own salaries. Looking at the low men on the major league totem pole, they can say, "Poor guys; they only make a few hundred thousand a year." It does seem meager, but the president of the United States only draws $400,000 a year. How many men in the whole of America would like to make $400,000 a year? Most would gladly change places with the lowest-paid man in either league.

Pitching, hitting, running, throwing, and a deep desire to play the game were at one time the essential ingredients of professional baseball players. In the major leagues' olden days, money was not *the* primary objective. Playing was. Outstanding players—the Ruths, Mantles, Williamses—had commanded astronomical salaries, upwards of $100,000 or a little more a year. Most of the other players were in a lower range, but all within sight of each other.

Thirty thousand dollars bought a fine house then and was, indeed, a higher than average salary. No player ever ventured on such an ego trip as to hold out for more money simply because he wasn't the highest paid player in the game. Minor leaguers were paid a pittance and managed to exist on it, always with the hope that in the next few years they would be taking home big-league pay.

Somewhere along the way, baseball rounded a corner and underwent a drastic monetary change. It has become a game of high stakes wherein good pitchers and sluggers make most of the nation's industrial leaders wish they could throw a baseball or swing a bat. Players still run, throw, hit, and slide, and they are still experts at scratching, spitting, spotting pretty girls in the stands, and going grizzled for days without shaving. Please realize that our tongues are in our cheeks, and that we know *all* players aren't cast from that mold, but if Willard Mullins, the great cartoonist for *The Sporting News*, were still alive, that's the way he would draw them—with money sticking out of their pockets!

"Baseball is so complicated now," John Henry Moss said. "Reflecting on my half century of experience in the game, I am reluctant to draw any hard-and-fast conclusions on the direction the major leagues are headed, especially in the area of such huge salaries.

"There are so many factors concerned—swiftly moving technology, new ideas and occurrences, economic activities, television, and so on—that we can't stop or even slow the change in the game, but it appears to be clear to all baseball people that they must work hard to restructure the revenue and expenses of major league clubs. I do not believe there is any question of the validity of that statement.

"There are so many factors in the evolution of this thing," John Henry added, "that I don't believe anyone who has spent a long time in professional baseball would want to make any statement of totality. It is my belief that there must soon be some very serious, innovative thought processes to restructure the whole financial aspect of baseball. The time has come when all involved should sit down and begin to work this thing out."

Rising ticket prices and increased travel expenses force the average fan to attend fewer games than he ordinarily would. A man who lives in, say, the Charlotte area, taking his wife and two kids to Atlanta for a weekend of baseball, figuring travel, hotel, food, tickets, and refreshments and souvenirs at the park, would have to fork out several hundred dollars for the trip, and this figure limits thousands of fans' visits to the Braves to once or twice a year. It is the same in other major league areas. That hard-working, blue-collared fan once was the backbone of baseball's support group. He is still important, but high-priced sky boxes and elevated ticket, concession, and souvenir prices have shifted this backbone of support to business and industry that can afford to buy season tickets and distribute them to employees, suppliers, buyers, and friends.

When Turner Field was opened in Atlanta a decade ago, Ted Turner, former owner of the Braves, was asked on television about the high price of beer in the stadium. "Why are they charging four dollars and a half for a beer?" a reporter asked.

"Four-fifty?" Turner looked surprised. "I wouldn't pay four-fifty for a beer!"

"We have to keep prices competitive," Moss explained. "As we speak, Major League Baseball has the lowest admission prices of any big league sport in the country, but the game still needs a readjustment."

Moss then looked toward his own South Atlantic League, a Class A circuit, and enumerated many changes taking place on that level.

"There will be a lot of new technology applied in the near future," he said. "I have had meetings with people of high technology on the digital process on our message boards. We are getting rid of those painted signs on the outfield fence, replacing them with digital message boards like those in the majors, which serve as scoreboard, message board, and advertising outlet. This is the direction the minor leagues are moving in."

The minors, of course, are dependent on the major leagues for their livelihood. Few minor league teams could make it on their own today, making their health and welfare dependent on that of the major leagues. By the same token, the majors rely on the minors to develop players to keep the level of major league play high.

"Ultimately the answers to our problems in the majors are going to have to be found," Moss said. "Ownership of all clubs must receive a return on their investments. Somehow the majors must work on this. And this must also reflect on better play afield for those clubs that seldom make it to the playoffs. If I go, say, six years without being in the playoffs, then I'm going to have to be given some special rules or considerations that will permit me to become competitive again.

"The answers to baseball's woes seem to be pretty clear," Moss said, "but how to implement them is the stickler. No one has come up with a way yet. I do not know how this can be worked out, but this is the computer age and with all the things we can do now, the human equation must find a way to accommodate all that technology."

For a moment, John Henry Moss put himself in someone else's shoes. "If I were a sports writer today," he said, "I would want to do some digging and write a story examining the payroll of a sports team—one from the National Basketball Association, the National Football League, the National Hockey League, or Major League Baseball. I wouldn't be looking for sensationalism, only for how salaries are paid. This would be one of the most exciting and revealing stories I could imagine.

"Somebody gets $90 million in salary over a period of years. Some of it is in deferred payment, and so on. Some of the major league clubs may still be paying salary to players who retired four or five years previously. That has happened already in a number of instances. This all becomes a liability of the operating corporation, so that individual who receives the money has a responsibility to the taxing agencies, and so would his heirs, in the case of an early death, of course.

"All of this is a very, very complicated process, which may be forcing some clubs, who try to stay reasonably competitive, to pay salaries today that they won't be able to afford to pay on down the road.

"Now, here's another thing: I don't hear baseball people talk about this because they shy away from it, but I do hear people wonder why teams can't help the smaller market clubs reach parity.

"Paying all income into the league and dividing it equally is impossible, could even be disastrous, and no doubt would remove a lot of incentive from the teams in larger market areas. I do hear people wonder why the clubs don't pool money they receive from television, but that is an enormous amount of their income. Unfortunately, the pooling of money tends to take away or reduce industriousness.

"I don't know where the answers to parity lie—maybe somewhere in what we've been talking about, or somewhere over the rainbow—but something has to be done to get the smaller teams moving," John said.

Moss feels major league teams are getting more competitive due to free agency and the upward movement of talented young players. Some teams that have not been winners in recent years suddenly become more competitive. Some examples are the revival of Minnesota, the Chicago Cubs, and the Phillies.

"Some people like to sleep late. Branch Rickey was not one of them," Moss said. "Any club that gets out and really works at it could put a good product on the field. So, really, what we need is more industriousness on the part of teams in smaller markets.

"Look how the game has changed: Mr. Rickey started the farm system in St. Louis in the 1930s when he owned the Cardinals. He had thirty-three minor league ball clubs feeding the Cardinals. No wonder they were dominant in the National League for a decade!

"Thirty-three teams is more than four eight-team leagues! What do you think would happen if a major league team had thirty-three minor league teams feeding it today? I guess they'd find it hard to pay some of the millions of dollars in salaries they're paying now.

"Of course, there is a lot more money around today. It brings to mind the amount of pay in days gone by, but in my lifetime. I know one guy who played in the Western Carolina League who's still carrying around his playoff check from years ago. It was for $1.74." That was Mel Roberts, who lived in the Spartanburg area and passed away in 2007. He was a veteran minor league manager and former coach for the Philadelphia Phillies and Atlanta Braves.

Chapter 13
A SECOND LIFE FOR THE WCL

Even after the Continental League dissolved, John Moss had no qualms about whether the Western Carolina League would operate that season of 1960. Franchises were ready to play in Lexington, Salisbury, Hickory, Newton-Conover, Shelby, Rutherford County, Statesville, and Gastonia, all in North Carolina.

Moss knew that a minor league could not last long, however, without major league support, so he set about the task of affiliating his teams. He attended the Winter Meetings in Louisville and began making contact with American and National League clubs on a one-on-one basis.

"We had a lot of image," he said, "because of our association with the Continental League and Mr. Rickey and the people around him, so we had good recognition and identity factors."

Houston apparently knew that it would soon become a major league city and Moss kept Houston aligned with his team in Salisbury. This was a simple paper transaction since Houston had agreed to work with Salisbury before the Continental League folded.

At those meetings Moss was able to talk seven major league clubs into lending some support to the WCL. Carl Hubbell, farm director for the San Francisco Giants, agreed to affiliate with Lexington, and the Giants sent outstanding prospect Bobby Bonds to play for Salisbury in 1960.

Moss then lined up the California Angels to work with Statesville and Pittsburgh to work with Gastonia. "That was a networking thing," Moss said. "Pittsburgh was affiliated with nearby Asheville, and I knew that Bob Clements, Pittsburgh's farm director, had married Tugga Wilson, a Gastonia girl whose father was a Ford dealer. I figured that would be a good connection, and it was. So Pittsburgh agreed to do limited work with Gastonia.

"We didn't get all eight of our clubs affiliated, but we got players from the major league farm systems for all eight. That's the way we went for three or four years, without formal agreements for all our teams, but I was able to get player assistance for all. Our clubs paid the salaries of players put on loan to them by the majors." Farm directors agreed to provide players because they had young men developing whose league or club had fallen out of baseball.

The Western Carolina League made it through the 1960 season in fairly good shape, but Hickory, Rutherford County, and Gastonia dropped out before the 1961 season. (The rapidly growing city of Hickory, which played the 1960 season, rejoined the league in 1993 with a new stadium and a new name—the Crawdads.) Moss talked the Giants into helping a new 1961 franchise in the tiny town of Belmont, outside Charlotte, and the Western Carolina operated with six teams—Lexington, Salisbury, Newton-Conover, Shelby, Statesville, and Belmont.

The assistance provided by the majors was only partial at that time, and the WCL clubs signed some players on their own. These, of course, were the property of the WCL teams.

"That created something of a problem," Moss said. "Some of our clubs would tinker with statistics at times, inflating batting averages, runs batted in, earned run averages, and other statistics

President John Henry Moss presents Hickory Crawdads president and principal owner Don Beaver with the South Atlantic League champion-ship trophy at the conclusion of the 2002 SAL playoffs.

on players they owned, hoping this would help bring a better price if they could sell them to the majors. This brought hard cash into the coffers. But it also created a rub with some of the major league teams. Western Carolina League team managers sometimes played their own players and let players on loan from the majors sit on the bench. Those teams were owned by pretty sharp businessmen, but what they did became a problem for the league."

John talked with Jack Schwartz, farm director of the Giants, who agreed to send some minor leaguers to the WCL. "Call me back later," Schwartz said, "and we'll work out details."

These players went to Belmont. In time, Schwartz called Moss and complained that Jim Poole, the Belmont manager, who had once played first base for Connie Mack's Philadelphia Athletics, was playing his own team's players at the expense of the Giants' farm hands. Schwartz sent Tim Murchison, his Carolinas area scout, to Belmont to investigate, and Murchison reported that Poole was indeed leaving the Giants players on the bench and playing his own.

"We're not putting players and equipment into Belmont," Schwartz told Moss, "to have our players cool their heels on the bench." John checked it and, to his chagrin, the Giants were right.

Some cases were rather severe. Phil Howser, who operated the Charlotte Hornets, a longtime affiliate of the Washington Senators, sent four players to Belmont, including Tony Oliva, a sure-fire prospect who later became a lifetime .304 hitter and three times American League batting champion with the Minnesota Twins. Poole had Oliva on the bench and was playing a big kid of his own. Oliva resented it and almost quit baseball, threatening to return home to Cuba. John Moss tightened his own screws on Poole and forced the manager to put Oliva in the lineup to pacify the Senators.

"This was not as one-sided as it may sound," John said. "Jim Poole was not an arch criminal. The major leagues were also playing games with our clubs. Howser and Clark Griffith, who owned the Senators, were sending their rookies to us so they could play with an organized team for a month until the Rookie League opened early in June. Oliva played for Belmont until the Rookie League opened, and then he was sent by the Senators to Wytheville, Virginia, in the Appalachian League."

In early December of 1961, six minor leagues asked for help from major league farm directors. Representatives of seventeen major league teams met with George Trautman to try to iron out problems for the six minor leagues' teams. The leagues were the Southern Association, the Three-I League, Northwest League, New York-Pennsylvania League, the Western Carolina League, and the Sophomore League. The problem for the Southern Association was that Atlanta and Birmingham, two of its original teams since 1902, had dropped out. Atlanta, growing rapidly toward major-league size, quit the league to move into the AAA International League, and Birmingham's franchise became a victim of the city's ban on integrated sports.

It was too late to save the Southern Association, the Three-I, and the Sophomore League, and all three dropped out of baseball after those meetings. The other three leagues managed to play the following season, albeit with problems.

In the December 6, 1961, issue of *The Sporting News*, Oscar Kahan reported, "When that meeting broke up, nothing had been accomplished." Dan Daniel, veteran sports writer for the *New York World-Telegram and Sun*, who had covered conventions of the National Association (the minor leagues) for more than forty years, wrote, "This is the most confused and disordered mess I've ever seen."

So the year of 1962 was a rough one for the minors. The fold up of the Southern Association created something of a chain reaction through the minors. The South Atlantic League, also an old-timer dating to 1904, absorbed some of the Southern Association's strongest cities and a year later, in 1963, moved up from Class A to AA status and became a truly thriving league.

The Western Carolina League lost two more teams for the 1962 season and had to play with only four clubs: Salisbury, Newton-Conover, Shelby, and Statesville. "That was one of the low periods in the minor leagues," John said. "It was pretty rocky, but I felt we finished the season in the strongest position of our league's three-year life. Despite the fact that we had only four clubs, I felt that the ones we had were stronger than ever and would give fans a better brand of baseball. I knew we were in the best position for major league assistance than in any year since we came back into baseball."

One reason for John's optimism was that seven big-league teams—the Yankees, Reds, Mets, Senators, Pirates, Dodgers, and Orioles—had sent players to the WCL's four teams that summer, elevating the brand of play considerably.

Between the 1962 and 1963 seasons, the major leagues finally decided to do something to strengthen the minors. Baseball had reached the point that no major league team could afford to operate a host of minor league farm teams.

Before that, league classifications had run AAA, AA, A, B, C, D, and R for Rookie. For a few years there was an "O" ranking for the Pacific Coast League, moving it one notch ahead of the AAA International League and American Association, ostensibly preparing the PCL to build itself into a third major league. Owners realized then, because of the strength of the Dodgers and Giants, that the Pacific Coast was major-league country. Before the 1963 season began, the majors completed restructuring, and the minors were limited to AAA, AA, A, and R leagues.

The majors had needed minor-league reclassification as badly as the minors. Big league clubs found it necessary to cut budgets in the face of rising costs, and this meant limiting the number of minor league teams each supported. So the majors ruled that each team could have only one AAA team, one AA team, one High A team and one Low A team, one short-season team, and one rookie team. This put all major league teams on a measure of parity inasmuch as no one could have more minor league affiliates than another.

"In no way did restructuring take initiative away from any minor league club," Moss said. "Actually, it stabilized the minor leagues. It was a consensus agreement that to solidify the minor league structure it was necessary to make these adjustments. Several minor leagues, like ours, had been bouncing back and forth with four, six, and eight clubs."

Under its new classification, 1963 was a banner year for the WCL. It returned to eight-team strength with the addition of three former South Atlantic League teams in Spartanburg, Rock Hill, and Greenville, all in South Carolina. That prompted adding an "s" to *Carolina*, making the league officially the *Western Carolinas League.* That year it consisted of Lexington, Salisbury, Shelby, Statesville, and Gastonia in North Carolina plus the three new South Carolina cities, which had better facilities and larger market areas than the previous WCL towns.

That move began a vast change in league makeup that would elevate it to one of the largest leagues in baseball and bring about a change in the league's name. The changes in league makeup the next few years were so great that not even the three South Carolina cities that started the change remained in the league.

Moss said the Western Carolinas League should be called the New Look League because it would be the most compact league in the country, with no road trip longer than ninety miles and no team having to make overnight trips, saving thousands of dollars in hotel expenses.

This was the beginning of four decades of amazing growth that has made the league one of the strongest minor leagues. Its caliber of baseball improved immediately with its uplift from Class D to Class A status. Major league farm systems that had been overstocked with ballplayers had to cull their minor league rosters, leaving only the best talent and prospects. Reclassification left some major teams with fewer minor league clubs, making better players available for Class A teams.

"One of our strengths at that time," John Moss said, "was our ability to get good publicity in the newspapers in our towns. There weren't that many other major professional sports to compete for space on the sports pages. We were getting good space in Charlotte, Asheville, and Winston-Salem, which were just on the borders of the Western Carolina League, and when we added the South Carolina cities, that gave us extra major newspaper publicity in Greenville, Rock Hill, and Spartanburg.

"I remember I used to send collect telegrams to Jake Wade, sports editor of the *Charlotte Observer*," John said. "I would wire Jake collect with things we wanted in the paper, and he would always run the items for us. But someone must have gotten onto him about it. He wrote a nice note and asked me just to call the *Observer* collect rather than sending news by telegraph."

Moss and the league received good press all over. On Sunday,

January 6, 1963, Ken Alexander quoted Moss in the *Gastonia Gazette* as saying the WCL would be stronger because the clubs could carry more veteran ballplayers and fewer rookies than before. Of Moss himself, Alexander wrote, "They said it couldn't be done in 1959 when John Henry put plans in motion for a WCL return the next year, after an absence of seven years. He struggled through 1960 as the ill-fated Continental League offered promise for the future, but then failed. Even after the WCL's strength was reduced to four teams last summer, Moss refused to throw in the towel and came out fighting. Now, with the realignment in baseball, there's a silver lining for Moss and his beloved WCL. The man from Kings Mountain deserves it."

Chapter 14
AN UNLIMITED FUTURE

For his work in reestablishing and rebuilding the Western Carolina League, John Henry Moss received accolades from many sources, including the highest-ranking baseball press. *The Sporting News*, published in St. Louis to cover both the major and minor leagues, ran a long story on Moss in its March 16, 1963, issue. Under the by-line of the *Gastonia Gazette's* Ken Alexander, who was a stringer for *The Sporting News,* the story was headlined "Battler Moss Builds Shaky Loop Into Muscular Minor," and a subhead read "Prexy of Western Carolinas Lands Backing of Majors, Doubles Size to 8 Clubs."

The story read:

> When it comes to organization, John Henry Moss will stand toe-to-toe with the best of them.
>
> That's the reason the Western Carolinas wasn't wrapped in black crepe a long time ago and laid out alongside other deflated minor baseball leagues.
>
> He's its president and, as you would expect, its biggest supporter.
>
> Prexy Moss is an optimist in every sense of the word. Nothing's impossible, he'll tell you.
>
> And after keeping the Western Carolinas alive against overwhelming odds, it's difficult to find arguing room with the North Carolinian.
>
> Right now he's in the process of shaping plans for the 1963 season which the energetic, hard-working president insists "will be the best Class A operation anywhere."
>
> This is typical of Moss. Since his amateurish start as a baseball leader back in 1946 in his native Kings Mountain, John Henry has lived by positive thinking.
>
> "That's the only way to be successful," he maintained. "Take the negative approach and you'll be a loser every time."

In his attempt to put the Western Carolinas on a firm footing, Moss has had more comebacks than Sugar Ray Robinson.

He refused to quit and, as a result, the Western Carolinas has withstood criticism, poor gates in a lot of instances, and a drop to a four-team operation in 1962.

But recognizing a "champion" when they see one, major league club owners have moved in to support one of the most amazing men in baseball today.

The WCL's lineup for 1963 includes Gastonia, Shelby, Lexington, Salisbury, and Statesville, all North Carolina clubs; and three Palmetto entries, Rock Hill, Greenville, and Spartanburg.

That's doubling the size of the operation of 1962, the year when critics felt Moss and his league had "had it."

Amazing, you say? Not if you know John Henry Moss.

Interviewing Eddie Gilliland, field representative for the National Association of Minor League Baseball, Neale Patrick wrote in the *Gastonia Gazette*:

> The Western Carolinas already was the most compact league in baseball. The travel hops are short and this makes it attractive to major league clubs wishing to place farm clubs. They don't like overnight trips for the low minors. Geographically, the Western Carolinas can't be beat.
>
> I prefer to see the lower minors to the Triple-A clubs. In the low classifications, you see the young players on the way up. But in the high minors, a lot of the players are not going anywhere and are just going through the motions.

The *Spartanburg Herald* called Moss "the Marco Polo of the minor league system," a reference to the fact that Moss would go anywhere if he could better his league, or even one team.

The Western Carolinas League's four-team operation in 1962 averaged an attendance of 19,345 per club for the season. In 1963, operating as an eight-team league, its average club attendance increased 150 percent to an average season attendance of 49,504 per city.

While on the subject of attendance, it should be noted that Spartanburg, which has always been a good baseball town, later became the first WCL team in history to draw more than 100,000 for a season. In 1965, the Spartanburg Phillies welcomed 114,796 fans, leading all Class A teams in baseball, and the next year it jumped to 173,010. Spartanburg drew more than 100,000 four straight years in the middle 1960s.

The Western Carolinas League settled down as a league after it reached eight teams in 1963, having between six and eight teams as franchises were changed until 1975, when it played two more years with four teams. However, they played an interlocking schedule, which gave the appearance of an eight-team league. In 1979, it grew back to six teams and in 1980 to eight. In 1982, it reached ten teams. Since that time, under John Henry's steady leadership, it has continued to grow until it reached sixteen teams in 2001.

Its future appears to be unlimited.

For his work with the Western Carolinas League in 1963, Moss received the Will Wynne Award at the annual meeting of the Raleigh chapter of the National Hot Stove League. The award was

Longtime Los Angeles Dodgers manager Tommy Lasorda tells a story to John Henry Moss at the Winter Meetings.

given each year to the person selected by North Carolina sports writers and sportscasters as having contributed the most to the game of baseball. The award was made on Monday, January 27, 1964. Previous winners had included Billy Goodman, Boston Red Sox; Hoyt Wilhelm, New York Giants; Whitey Lockman, New York Giants; Enos (Country) Slaughter, New York Yankees; Tommy Byrne, New York Yankees; Roger Craig, Los Angeles Dodgers; and Smoky Burgess, Pittsburgh Pirates. Moss was the first nonplayer to win the cup.

At the early 1964 convention of the National Association in San Diego, Ford Frick, commissioner of baseball, congratulated John Moss on "the tremendous strides he has taken since becoming president of the Western Carolinas League in 1960. Minor League Baseball is on the upswing in the United States," said Frick, "and the success of the major leagues depends on the success of the minors."

Everyone in baseball wanted to pat John Moss on the back. No one had ever done a more thorough job of building and rebuilding a league of any classification.

Other honors rolled his way as the years passed. Moss was named King of Baseball in 1990, and three years later was given the prestigious Warren E. Giles Award, which recognized his outstanding service as a league president. He has also served as chairman of the Executive Committee of the National Association of Professional Baseball Leagues, Inc., as well as vice chairman of the Council of League Presidents.

No one could ever accuse John Moss of not having given his all to promotion and development of baseball in the South.

Chapter 15
GROWING PAINS

In 1964, the South Atlantic League changed its name to the Southern League when it began bringing in some of those old Southern Association cities of Birmingham and Chattanooga, and later Knoxville and Nashville. The South Atlantic League had on occasion been known as the Sally League, perhaps originally for brevity in newspaper headlines.

There was no Sally League from 1964 until 1980, and then it reappeared in the record books. The reason was that the Western Carolinas League was moving southward in South Carolina and Georgia and would soon take in five of the six original towns of the Sally—Charleston, South Carolina (joined in 1973), and Macon, Georgia (1980), Columbia, South Carolina (1983), Savannah, Georgia (1984), and Augusta, Georgia (1988), missing only Jacksonville, Florida, which had become a member of the AAA International League in 1962. So, for the 1980 season, the Western Carolinas League voted to drop its name and revert to the name South Atlantic League.

Gone were the North Carolina teams from Lexington, Salisbury, Newton-Conover, Shelby, Rutherford County, Statesville, and Belmont. Spartanburg, Rock Hill, and Greenville, the South Carolina franchises that helped the WCL with its greatest expansion, were no longer members.

Through the 1960s and 1970s, towns like Thomasville, Monroe, and Charlotte in North Carolina, and Orangeburg, in South Carolina, became members of the league for a while and then dropped out, some going on to higher leagues and others disappearing from professional baseball. The 1980s saw a few teams come and go. Florence, Greenwood, Sumter, Anderson, and Myrtle Beach, South Carolina, and Shelby and Fayetteville, North Carolina, played a while and left.

Then in the 1990s and for three years in the twenty-first century, Moss changed some teams to give the league a solid sixteen-team roster divided into Northern and Southern divisions. The divisions play interlocking schedules.

The number of teams dwindled for a while, and then the league took in more cities to increase in size. Aside from 1975 and 1976 when only four clubs operated, it was a six-team league from 1967 through 1979. In 1980, there were eight teams again until 1986 when two new cities made it a ten-team league. In 1989, it became a twelve-team circuit, and in 1991 it grew to fourteen, and on to sixteen in 2001.

Now the South Atlantic League stretches into eight states: North and South Carolina, Georgia, Maryland, West Virginia, Kentucky, Ohio, and New Jersey—and no longer do teams get to spend every night in their own beds. Expanding geography dictates that all teams have to spend some nights on the road. Under the minors' reclassification, the Sally League is thriving.

"We had to grow into larger cities," Moss said. "It was an impossible task keeping alive with country towns when such leagues as the Southern Association and others were dying."

The name change in 1980 from Western Carolinas League to South Atlantic League was also geographically necessitated. Moss said, "Half of our cities—Charleston, Spartanburg, Anderson, and Macon—were from South Carolina or Georgia, and the South Atlantic League seemed to be the best name for us. The name had a broader scope in baseball. It was a name everybody recognized, and we felt justified in changing names, if for no other reason than to hold onto a great deal of Minor League Baseball history."

Moss added, "In 2001 when we expanded to sixteen teams, we took our place at the front of the line in the minor leagues."

The name of the South Atlantic League is also truer than the name of the Western Carolinas League, because the new league reaches into five seaboard states on the Atlantic Ocean—Georgia, South Carolina, North Carolina, Maryland, and New Jersey— and the others—Kentucky, Ohio, and West Virginia—aren't that far removed.

Chapter 16
MAYOR JOHN HENRY MOSS

The lead paragraph of a feature story on Mayor John Henry Moss of Kings Mountain in the *Asheboro (N.C.) Courier-Tribune* on December 12, 1975, read:

> Kings Mountain had not recorded a "major victory" since 1780 when the American militia defeated Major Patrick Ferguson of the British army at Kings Mountain in a battle that marked a turning point in the American Revolution—that is, not until 1965 when John Henry Moss won the race for mayor.

It was in Kings Mountain in 1780 that sharp-eyed, straight-shooting mountain men descended from the forest fastnesses of the North Carolina wilderness to hand the British a devastating defeat. A thousand grizzled mountain men whipped Maj. Patrick Ferguson and the British Redcoats and brought the American Revolution to a swifter conclusion.

Over the span of the next twenty-three years, John Henry Moss's victory was a $40 million triumph over Kings Mountain's poverty and lethargy. The dynamic Mr. Moss was considered one of the most progressive mayors in North Carolina in his twelve terms of office from 1965 to 1988.

During that period, Moss secured more than $40 million in federal grants for Kings Mountain and was written up in *Time* and *U.S. News and World Report*, and featured on a three-minute spot on the *CBS Evening News* and on *60 Minutes* for having secured more federal grant revenues per capita than any other city official in the United States.

"When you play in that league," John Moss said, "you always wonder whether you did something right or wrong. The *Evening News* was so positive that I figured what I had done must have been all right, and now I'm going to play hard in both leagues." He kept his job as president of the Western Carolinas League because he felt he had many more things to accomplish on the baseball diamond.

John, whose political career had included only a stint as town commissioner in Kings Mountain, had only one goal when he decided to run for mayor: to help the citizens of his town of some eight thousand advance themselves on the plane of good living. Having earned a reputation as a go-getter from his astute building of the WCL into a strong member of the dwindling number of minor baseball leagues, Moss turned his attention to politics with a fervor.

He loved a challenge of any sort. He had first encountered such a challenge as a bodyguard assigned to protect high-ranking American military officials in Europe during World War II, and next he encountered the task of rebuilding a baseball league that he had birthed and that had been shattered by excessive spending and had laid dormant for seven years. He thought of the mayoral challenge as perhaps the biggest, or at least the most meaningful,

As mayor of Kings Mountain, John Henry Moss receives a City of Excellence certificate from North Carolina Governor Jim Hunt. Moss was dubbed the Mayor with the Midas Touch because of his successful fundraising on behalf of the city.

because it concerned the betterment of living conditions for his life-long friends and neighbors.

With the baseball league back on its feet and promising huge progress in future years with the inclusion of the strong South Carolina cities of Greenville, Spartanburg, and Rock Hill, John Henry had felt it time to answer the call to help his town lift itself out of the doldrums.

He put his name in the hat for the mayoral race, and in the municipal election of May 11, 1965, polled 1,242 votes to ten-year incumbent Glen A. Bridges' 671 and former mayor Kelly Dixon's 108 votes. With almost a two-to-one margin, Moss rode into office on a landslide that continued to roll for twenty-four years.

Before he was elected, Moss pledged his efforts toward a progressive Kings Mountain. Kings Mountain allowed each elected mayor to fill the office either part time or full time. When he was elected, John Henry opted for the full-time mayoral office. "I want to give this job everything I have," he said. "It's going to take a lot of time and effort to do the job I have in mind, and I am determined to do it."

His first task, he thought, was to tackle poverty, and he reasoned the best way to win that battle would be to bring jobs to Kings Mountain and Cleveland County. He sought industry, and after a period of persistent digging, probing, and cajoling, that facet of his work began to bring forth fruit.

Forming an industrial development corporation of influential citizens, he secured a four-hundred-acre tract in northeast Kings Mountain for the purpose of locating an industrial park with stated prices for sites and arrangements for the physical facilities industry required, such as water, power, gas, and rail and highway access. This, he felt, took the guesswork out of the area's industry-seeking effort. Since 1957, the town had been involved in seeking industry on a small scale and had registered some success, but Moss's plan was to attack the problem on a wider front, and his efforts began to pay off.

The *Daily Star*, from the neighboring town of Shelby, reported on August 31, 1965:

During his political campaign, Moss pledged his efforts toward a progressive Kings Mountain. Now, four months after election, Kings Mountain is on the verge of acquiring several new industries, which could employ more than five hundred persons; revitalizing its downtown business district through a multimillion dollar urban renewal project; updating its antiquated zoning laws; and setting its sights on a bright economic future.

"I try to run Kings Mountain like a man runs a successful corporation," John Moss said, "but I also must remember I represent the people."

Moss named 80 percent of downtown landowners to a Mayor's Committee for Downtown Development aimed toward turning the downtown area into a shopping mecca. The resulting plan called for refronting most stores, creating thousand-car parking lots, the closing of streets, and building of pedestrian malls. The plan was approved.

The first plant to locate in the industrial park was J. E. Herndon Company, a Kings Mountain cotton waste firm that was rebuilding after a fire. In the first three years of his office, Moss also brought in such manufacturers as Kinder Manufacturing Company of Elkhart, Indiana, the largest mobile home industry in America; Dependable Knit, Inc., a circular knit operation for outerwear and sportswear; and Oxford Industries of Atlanta, which built the thirty-seventh plant in its chain in Kings Mountain, a 200,000-square-foot facility that manufactured knit shirts and sweaters. It eventually employed seven hundred persons.Over the years since then, Moss and his committees attracted more industry until the entire county found itself moving back onto its feet.

At the completion of his two-year term in 1967, Moss won reelection as an unopposed incumbent, the first since 1921. The *Kings Mountain Herald* of April 27, 1967, reported:

> None can fairly assess the fact of minimal political activity this year without crediting the energy, imagination, hard work, and dedication of Mayor John Henry

Moss, the city's chief executive officer. . . .

A few items of evidence: (1) successful presentation of the sewage system bond issue, favored by the voters 42 to 1; (2) launching of a long-term water program which will benefit the whole area and, for water, Eastern Cleveland County, particularly; (3) expansion of the city recreation department; (4) efforts at city cleanup; (5) attention to low-rent housing for the poor who qualify. Meantime, the normal work of the city—from fire protection to garbage pickups—was continued at full measure.

All the time Moss was working for the improvement of Kings Mountain, he continued to hold the office of president of the Western Carolinas League, which became the South Atlantic League during his term as mayor, and continued to prosper and grow.

All of Moss's time in the mayor's chair was not pure sweat and hard work. He also found time to let the city play. Its largest ever festivity came in 1965, five months after Moss took office. He engineered a 185th anniversary celebration of the Battle of Kings Mountain, which Thomas Jefferson had regarded as having turned the tide of the American Revolution toward victory for the colonies. The battle was noted as the first in a series of setbacks that ended in the collapse of the British struggle to hold America.

This celebration was a big affair, which was exactly what John Moss planned it to be. He wanted Kings Mountain to receive as much publicity as possible—and a lot of fun for everyone—from a celebration of this sort. Festivities were scheduled for October 9, 1965. The actual battle had taken place on the mountain on October 7, 1780, but the ninth fell on Saturday, the best day of the week for such an undertaking.

The festivities went on for an entire week, and more than twenty-five hundred persons marched in the parade that started the Saturday event. A crowd of forty thousand watched, including fifty invited dignitaries who filled a viewing box on Railroad Avenue.

Maj. Gen. Joe S. Lawrie, commanding general of Fort Bragg, was grand marshal of the parade. Miss South Carolina of 1965, Nancy Moore of North Aiken (who later married South Carolina Senator Strom Thurmond) was the featured attraction in the parade.

Following the parade, Park Superintendent Ben F. Moomaw of the Kings Mountain Battlefield was master of ceremonies at the Kings Mountain National Military Park. Secretary of the Army Stanley R. Resor was the featured speaker. On hand were senators, congressmen, beauty queens, state and local officials, and the governors of North and South Carolina. Both had baseball backgrounds. Dick Riley, the South Carolina governor, had been batboy for the Greenville Spinners in the South Atlantic League years before, and Jim Hunt, North Carolina's governor, was a batboy for the Wilson Cobs in the Carolina League in bygone days.

The U. S. Army's 82nd Airborne Division's skydiving team, the Golden Knights, jumped nine men from an airplane at 13,500 feet. They descended against a backdrop of a glowing gold and vermillion sunset in baton-passing, crossovers, and accuracy maneuvers as they free-fell for 8,000 feet. When they popped open their chutes a sudden vicious wind blew five of them off course, but the other four landed within fifty yards of their target. The same team returned

John Henry Moss was a guest in the mid-1970s on the popular television show *Good Morning Carolina*, which aired on WSOC-TV, Channel 9, in Charlotte. Moss is pictured with host Brad Lacey.

the following year for a similar celebration, did the same jump, and all landed on the target dead center.

The day ended with the celebration's grand ball at the armory and with rock 'n' roll street dancing on Railroad Avenue.

At the 186th anniversary the following year, the U. S. Navy, not to be outdone by the army, which had supplied the featured speaker the year before, sent Secretary of the Navy Paul H. Nitze to do the job. Kings Mountain learned from that celebration that its mayor did things on a grand scale and looked for more.

"Our celebration was a huge success," Moss said. "Such festivities had been held periodically for about seventy-five years, but I believe ours ranked with or ahead of any of them."

Kings Mountain had a city hall but no special room for meetings of the town board, so the town formed a makeshift chamber by pushing together two tables in the courtroom at City Hall. The *Asheboro Courier-Tribune* noted that of the seven town mayors in Cleveland County, only John Moss stood erect to preside over meetings of the town board. "Perhaps this is symbolic of his drive to get Kings Mountain 'on its feet' and moving toward total development," the paper editorialized.

John and Elaine Moss hosted a drop-in party on December 28, 1969, for all Vietnam veterans, their wives, and the wives of men either killed in action or then serving in Vietnam. He called it one of the highlights of his career as mayor. At the party, the mayor met a man after his own heart, Roy Ruff, who had lost both legs in Vietnam. Ruff said he was glad to be a civilian again, but added that he would not trade his military experience for anything.

"It was encouraging to meet with those young people and find that they are so interested in the community," John said. "They seem more concerned with looking ahead than they are with their own personal problems."

One young wife commented, "Now that my husband's duty in Vietnam is past, we can begin planning for the future." And John replied, "That's what I hope to do for all these young people, help them plan their future."

As mayor, John Moss was nobody's fool. His brain was always working and his eyes forever looking ahead. His main campaign promise in all eleven elections he won was that he would devote his time, energy, and talents to give progressive leadership to the task of making Kings Mountain a better place to live. This was not merely a political promise from one seeking votes; it was John Henry's mandate to the people. They knew he meant what he promised, and he proved it term after term by coming up with new grants and masterminding new projects of all kinds.

John kept almost two hundred and fifty town residents working on committees, like the Mayor's Housing Committee, the Industrial Committee, the Bicentennial Commission, the Mayor's Summer Youth Employment Committee, and the Clean-up, Paint-up, Fix-up Committee. All committee heads and members were hand-picked by Moss himself.

"Everything he touches seems to turn to gold," an editor wrote in the *Kings Mountain Herald*, "especially if what he's touching turns out to be an application for federal aid. He has made grant-getting a science."

If an application for federal aid became snarled in Washington's red tape, Moss took the next airplane to the nation's capital and went about unsnarling the application with what he termed "plain old hard head-knocking." He could joust verbally with the best of the Washington crowd, and he felt no qualms in doing so, because he was working for the people. He stood by his campaign promises. He never had a "leg man" in Washington to push the grant applications through, but preferred to do the work himself.

The "Battle of Buffalo Creek" was so named by the *Shelby Daily Star* in its April 28, 1969, edition, when opposition surfaced against a Moss project to build a $3.3 million, 1,500-acre lake on Buffalo Creek. The lake was intended to solve Kings Mountain's water problems for time to come and to add more recreational facilities to those that Cleveland County already offered the public.

The *Star* reported that "in an uncharacteristic public display of temper, Mayor John Henry Moss, his voice shaking and hand trembling at first said, 'Thirty-six months of hard work have gone into this project. We have suffered many harassments, but we have tried to keep our chin high, and we think we have. All along the way some people have been pushing stumbling blocks into our path. We have endured this. . . . There comes a time for cooperation on both sides of Buffalo Creek.' A big bone of contention was who would have authority over the lake."

Apparently this helped quiet opposition to the project. Voters had approved the project by a 20-to-1 margin on December 6, 1967, and it was finished and opened on November 18, 1970. One newspaper, commenting later on the 1,500-acre lake, reported that it had "attracted private investors and is fast becoming one of the best residential and recreational areas in the state."

The *Asheboro Courier-Tribune* reported after Moss's first ten years in office:

> Some 14 times in the last 10 years Moss has gathered in a federal grant for Kings Mountain. A single grant last August totaled $4,160,000. All 14 grants have amounted to $16,383,196, or about $2,000 for every man, woman, and child in this Cleveland County community of just over 9,000.
>
> These federal grants have meant that Kings Mountain has been able to build a 31,000-square foot community center, a 1,500-acre lake that will take care of its water needs for the foreseeable future, and a facility that has increased the town's capacity for treating sewage from five thousand gallons to five million.
>
> Kings Mountain became the first city in North Carolina to employ a "scattered" public housing concept, whereby public housing is scattered throughout Kings Mountain's residential areas instead of in one big project.
>
> The latest grant for $4.16 million is a five-year contract from the U. S. Department of Housing and Urban Development (HUD). It includes 13 projects ranging from urban beautification to the development of child-care programs to programs for the handicapped and aged.

Looking back from the vantage point of many years down the road, John Moss beams with pride when he visits the lake, the waste treatment plants on McGill and Pilot creeks, the community facilities building, the various manufacturing plants that came into Kings Mountain, and the urban renewal projects in the town. He is especially proud of the fact that public housing was scattered throughout the town and of the pride that those who occupied the housing took in their new homes, keeping them attractive like the remainder of the neighborhood. "We didn't build a ghetto in Kings Mountain," he said. "We built homes."

John Henry Moss's efforts to improve life in Kings Mountain benefitted all who lived in the town, and they drew praise from people all across North Carolina, even reaching the Governor's Mansion, where in 1971 Gov. Bob Scott praised Moss for "tremendous progress . . . planned progress."

John left the mayor's office on December 15, 1988, a proud man for all the things his efforts had produced for Kings Mountain. He relinquished the mayor's chair because he felt he had done the job required of him, and he also needed to devote more time to baseball, with his SAL growing into one of the strongest and largest leagues in America.

Chapter 17
EXPANSION AND REBUILDING

By 1988, the new South Atlantic League contained five of the six original Sally League teams. After Charleston, South Carolina, joined the league in 1973, Macon came in in 1980, Columbus in 1983, Savannah in 1984, and Augusta in 1988. As the appeal of South Atlantic League baseball grew under the watchful eye of John Henry Moss, the league stretched its boundaries to Charleston, West Virginia, and to the Delmarva Peninsula with a team in Salisbury, Maryland.

To distinguish between the two SAL Charleston clubs, Charleston, South Carolina, became designated Charleston South and Charleston, West Virginia, was called Charleston West. The Charleston West team is now known as West Virginia Power, and the franchise is still based in Charleston.

Some cities had to rebuild or renovate their ballparks, such as Asheville's McCormick Field, which had opened in 1924. Those of other teams that came into the league had been constructed from the 1920s to the 1940s. "Beginning with Asheville," Moss said, "I met with ownership and the Buncombe County Board of Commissioners, which owned McCormick Field, where the Asheville Tourists had played since 1924, and through two or three meetings I strongly encouraged the development of the city's baseball facilities.

"How we approach this is vital," Moss added. "We use an appealing sales presentation on how baseball enhances the quality of life in a city by providing wholesome, affordable family entertainment, and this argument is honest and valid and is recognized as such in most cities.

"It is not hard for a governing body to do something the citizens want, so we first come into a town and sell the advantages of a large, comfortable ballpark to the people, who then convey their wishes to the governing body. We don't pull wool over anybody's eyes. Our arguments are honest, and people like what we present.

"From Asheville," Moss said, "I went to Macon where Luther Williams Field needed an upgrade. Finally, I went to Savannah to check out sixty-five-year-old historic Grayson Stadium, and they upgraded it."

In the 1990s, super stadiums began to appear in the SAL, beginning with a $19 million stadium in Charleston South with luxury suites and all the amenities of major league parks. The Atlanta Braves moved their franchise from Macon to Rome, Georgia, for the 2003 season and constructed a beautiful new minor league ballpark.

Moss recalled: "We have new stadiums in Charleston and Greenville, South Carolina; Charleston, West Virginia; Asheville, Greensboro, Hickory, and Kannapolis, North Carolina; Augusta, Columbus, and Rome, Georgia; the Delmarva Peninsula; Eastlake, New Jersey; Lexington, Kentucky; and Lake County, Ohio. That's fifteen new and modern facilities. We are working with Savannah, Georgia, and Hagerstown, Maryland, to build or expand and renovate their ballparks."

National Association President Sal Artiaga shakes hands with the catcher after throwing out the ceremonial first pitch in Greensboro, North Carolina, in 1990. Artiaga served as president from 1988 to 1991.

The Sally League has joined the major league progression of securing corporate names for stadiums. As of this writing, corporate sponsors' names are on new stadiums in Lakewood, Greenville, Rome, Greensboro, Kannapolis, Lake County, West Virginia, and Lexington.

Diehard baseball fans sometimes scoff at teams allowing their stadiums to be named after corporations, but if they were standing on the other side of the fence, they would discover a whole new attitude toward this. "When a club allows a corporation to name its stadium," Moss said, "there is more to it than just tagging on the name. In corporate naming, a club would think and negotiate in terms of $300,000 a year—that's a ballpark figure, if you'll excuse the pun—for ten years, which would give the team an income of $3 million over that span.

"The new and renovated parks," Moss stresses, "need sky boxes,

In 1950, John Moss handled the color commentary for the Richmond Red Devils High School basketball games on WKBV in Richmond, Indiana.

or luxury suites, like the majors have, a picnic area, a restaurant that's open every day of the year, and a good salesroom in the stadium where memorabilia is sold, including tee-shirts, baseball caps, pennants, and such, and this part of the business should have counter agreements with outside outlets.

"The restaurant is important," Moss added. "In the new park in Lexington, they have a restaurant with white tablecloth service and folks have dinner there. The restaurant is open whether the team is in town or not, and serves as a good luncheon place for business people and a dinner site for all. West Virginia has a top-of-the-line restaurant with a chef who takes only one day off each year. In our stadium restaurants, we want the atmosphere to be pleasant, the food good, and there should be a lot of baseball memorabilia, or perhaps the restaurant could open on one side with a good view of the field and the inside of the stadium. That encourages new fans to come to the ballpark, and if you can get them there to eat, many of them will return for games. Regardless, a restaurant, properly operated, turns a good profit for the team."

John Henry also encourages his teams to develop radio broadcasts of their games, and to do this on the scale of a network of stations in smaller towns surrounding the market city. The Lexington, Kentucky, Sally League franchise has a twenty-station network carrying its team's games.

"A website is vital," Moss said. "All teams in the league have developed these to help keep the public informed on club activities, and they are paying off now. This is the same thing that Wal-Mart, Kmart, and other businesses use to determine their markets. That's where I have been trying to take our league's teams."

When Moss visits a town being considered for admission to the league, he does not go empty-handed.

"I don't go into a town," he said, "and advise it to build a stadium or do a major renovation on an older one for just seventy baseball games a year, which is the number of home games our teams play in a 140-game schedule. Other promotions should be held to put the ballpark in use a minimum of 110 times a year. That is a reasonable figure. This business pays off in many minor league cities, helping both the baseball club and the city.

"One thing I'm talking about is that there should be a minimum of other events in the park every year. These should include promotions of music shows and other events that can be held outdoors, large meetings of people, wrestling matches, shows like the Oak Ridge Boys, various things like that. A promotional sales force would have to be employed to generate this business, and a goal of 110 events is not at all unreasonable. It simply takes some work to do this."

That brought up another point.

"Clubs in our league," he said, "that employ all the things I have mentioned need a working force of more than twenty people to make maximum progress. The grounds crew needs a minimum of two-and-a-half people. Then you break it down like this: three people in front office administration, three or four in group sales, at least three in corporate sales, three in sponsorship sales, probably three in concessions, three or more in the store because of credit card sales and all that. Public relations would need three or four, which would include the team mascot, who needs to take the fun of the mascot outside the ballpark into schools and civic clubs. I envision a staff of about twenty-seven is needed to run a solid minor league operation."

Such operations have been successful in other leagues. For example, during the 2001 season, Lansing, Michigan, of the Midwest League, which has the same classification as the South Atlantic, drew 4,012 for a picnic, and on another evening had 12,654 people in the stands. Lansing's attendance for the season was 451,000.

"That's in Kane County," Moss said, "about fifty miles west of Detroit. That's what the marketing structure is doing today in the minor leagues. Columbia, South Carolina, which was one of our markets, has a little better demographics than Lansing, and we have five cities in our league larger than Columbia—Lexington, Greensboro, Columbus, Savannah, and Rome—and the two Charlestons and Augusta are growing rapidly, so one can readily see that the potential is in our league for similar operations."

For those who may not be able to put an exact definition to the word *demographics,* it is the statistical characteristics of human populations (as age and income) used especially to identify markets.

"This is a whole structured procedure," Moss said, "the same as if you were running a hospital or any other business. In a recent speech to a group of young executives, I asked how many in the audience had ever worked in a political campaign. A few hands went up. I asked how many were acquainted with the personnel director of an industry, or the hospital, or the school system. Other hands went up. I told them that's where they go for group sales and such as that. Working that way in a baseball operation, we are operating at a lot less than it costs to sell shoes."

The demographic is present in most South Atlantic League cities, some of whom have small city populations but possess metropolitan statistics when surrounding county statistics are figured. Asheville would be an example, with a city population of 70,000 but with a head count of more than 250,000 in Buncombe County, all of whom live within less than a half-hour drive of the city's baseball park.

The tarp to cover the field when it rains is one thing in baseball that still gives all minor league teams problems. "There is no easy way to get the tarp on the ground," Moss said. "In the few weeks of dog days in southern towns, when it rains quick showers of cats and dogs almost every day and night, we need to make quick work of covering the field. More people are needed to unroll and spread the tarp than minor league clubs can afford to have on their grounds crews.

"As long as I've been in baseball," Moss added, "I don't know what to say about handling the tarp. I can't say, 'Well, just let it rain the game out,' because ultimately that would get back to the big league team with a working agreement with the team we're talking about and would give the impression that that minor league town is not doing everything it can to give the parent club's players the opportunity to train and develop.

"One way to handle the tarp question would be to have some other employees come out and help with it, but the people who manage concessions are busy with selling and serving picnics, and you can't just drag people out of the stands to help. This is something that each individual club has had to work out."

Chapter 18
A Lifetime Job

It is an amazing thing what people like John Henry Moss have done for the minor leagues, for the progress they've made and for the plans they have, and John Henry stands at the head of the class. Baseball is in the process of patterning minor league clubs after major league operations, streamlining ballparks and marketing and front-office attitudes toward the game.

"John is a real politician," said Ron McKee, retired general manager and part-owner of the Asheville Tourists. "He is from the old school, but is a man with new ideas. When we had league meetings, he'd have people wait in the hallways while he ran things with protocol."

For many years of Moss's career as president of the league, his contract was for three years at a time. It expired on October 1 of the third year. He always asked for his three-year extension at such time that he would gain another year, which meant his contract really covered four seasons.

The league met in Nashville in 1999, when time had come to vote on John's contract again. When he brought the subject before the directors, McKee said, "If we're going to discuss John's salary and term of office, I would like for him to leave the room."

Ron chuckles when he thinks of that meeting. He was following protocol, John Henry style, to the *n*th degree, but John had never been asked to leave the room before. Renewal of his contract had always been an all-in-favor-say-aye rubber stamping.

"I had sometimes been critical of John," McKee explained, "never of his motives but sometimes of his methods. However, I think we all recognize that his methods are what got things done and really why the league is at such a high peak today."

When John left the room, several of the directors thought McKee might have a dump-John-Henry movement in mind, but

McKee put that notion quickly to rest. "I don't have anything particular in mind," Ron said, "but John has been president of this league for a long time. It is his life, and we are his children, and I think we ought to do something more special for him than elect him for three more years."

The directors concurred and began to talk about a trip to Hawaii for John and Elaine, and about a bonus, and about other ways to honor him for his service.

Suddenly, Ron said he felt words coming from his mouth that he had never thought of until that moment. He said, "Why don't we elect him league president for life?" Such a thing had never been done in a professional baseball league.

The directors began to discuss the idea. Someone said, "What if he becomes incapacitated?"

"Look, guys," Ron said, "the way we elect him now, it's for almost five years. Why not make it a lifetime contract?"

After some discussion, the lifetime contract came to a vote, and John Henry was elected to it by unanimous vote. McKee then said, "I want to tell him when he comes in. Don't anybody say a word."

The discussion had taken about a half hour, and all that time John was in the hall cooling his heels, wondering what in the world the directors were doing.

John Henry Moss is crowned the King of Baseball at the 1990 Winter Meetings in Los Angeles. The King of Baseball Award is given annually in appreciation for dedicated service to professional baseball.

McKee looked him squarely in the eye and in his sternest voice began, "Mr. Moss, your request for a three-year extension on your contract as president of the South Atlantic League has been denied."

John's chin dropped and no one in the room would look him in the eye.

Ron let that first statement sink in, and then said, "Instead, Mr. Moss, the board of directors of the South Atlantic League has elected you league president for life."

An ovation, filled with much laughter, broke out among the directors.

"It was fun," Ron said, "seeing his face drop like that, but he deserved the vote, and I don't think anything has ever pleased him more."

"It was something that really made him feel good," Ron related during a later interview. "John has amazing vitality, running up and down the roads all the time at his age—in his eighties—making two trips each year to every ballpark in the league, which sends him on thirty-two such excursions, with sixteen ballparks to visit."

Those are seldom easy visits, although John enjoys them tremendously. John's forman administrative assistant in the league office, Patrick Heavener, was his chauffeur, driving him back and forth on these visits, but Pat married and left the job, which is now filled in the office by a most efficient woman, Judy Carman.

On each visit to each club, John talks over the club's problems to the extent that it usually takes two days to complete a visit, and those clubs are scattered from South Georgia to New Jersey and as far west as Kentucky.

Moss also holds league meetings four times a year in various league cities, and these consume several days each in preparation for and actual work on location. Finally, the league holds its annual meeting and an awards dinner each year in a league city, handing out the season's awards for most valuable player, outstanding major league prospect, most outstanding pitcher, and for off-the-field honors such as sales executive of the year, general manager of the year, groundskeeper of the year, and so on.

Chapter 19
THE PAINS OF EXPANSION

Two of the current South Atlantic League teams were added in 2001, giving it a sixteen-team field. That did not occur by accident, but by design, and it was a distinct about-face from that ages-old attitude of letting minor leagues look out for themselves.

In the SAL, not any of the teams have to struggle to make ends meet. All draw sufficient attendance, coupled with advertising and memorabilia sales, to keep their heads above water, and in many cases to register a welcome profit.

Addition of the two clubs to the Sally League balanced the league, which offered several pluses, not the least of which was easier scheduling and less travel. Schedule makers find it easier to make schedules for leagues that number their teams in multiples of four, i.e. four, eight, twelve, sixteen.

At the Class A level of Organized Baseball there are two categories, called Low A and High A leagues. This does not mean that the Low A leagues offer less competition. It has only to do with length of professional service. Low A leagues are for players in their second and third years of professional baseball; High A leagues are for those in their third and fourth years. Many of the high bonus babies start out in the Low A leagues, where competition is just as tough as in High A.

The High A leagues are the Carolina, Florida State, and California leagues. The South Atlantic and Midwest leagues are Low A circuits.

The Florida State League uses the major leagues' spring training stadiums for their summer games, and the league gradually realized that it had a couple of clubs whose attendance did not hold up through the extremely hot summer months. Needing every league and every team to develop talent for the majors, the minors acted to bolster those less-drawing franchises. In St. Petersburg and

Kissimmee, the stadiums were usually filled for major league spring training games, but in the hot summer months attendance slacked off greatly for minor league play.

Under the structure of the A leagues in 2000, there were thirty-two High A teams and only twenty-eight Low A teams. Major league farm directors thought it would be better to have the A leagues balanced with thirty teams in High and thirty in Low, and that work was done. Today the balance is equal, making for a smoother operation at both levels, major and minor leagues.

They reached equality in high and low A teams when the powers that be telephoned John Moss and asked if his South Atlantic League could take on two new members, and John Henry immediately

John Henry Moss may have thrown out more ceremonial first pitches at ballparks throughout the country than anyone in the game.

answered, "Yes, we can do that. We can take in two more teams easily." He gave his answer before he talked to his league's directors, so sure was he that the league would approve the expansion.

Two good minor league cities, Lexington, Kentucky, and Montgomery, Alabama, were interested in membership in the Sally League. During negotiations, Montgomery dropped out of the running, and Wilmington, North Carolina, accepted the second expansion franchise. The Fayetteville Cape Fear Crocs were moved to Lakewood, New Jersey. The Wilmington Waves moved after one season to Albany, Georgia, and eventually became the Columbus Catfish.

Each city joined together enough affluent men and women to put up entrance fees of $3.5 million each, payable to the South Atlantic League. With this money, the Sally League purchased the two Florida State League teams. The Sally also compensated the Florida State with $400,000 to make up for the shortfall in its league dues. Obviously, the fewer teams the Florida State had, the less money it would have to operate the league office.

The Sally League netted some money from the overall deal, but not a lot.

This switch of minor league franchises set a precedent in baseball. It was the first time ever that minor leagues in the United States swapped franchises, even though the same had been done in major league cities as far back as the removal of the Braves from Boston to Milwaukee. Talk immediately rose of taking two low-drawing franchises out of the California League and placing them in other cities in the Carolina League. This would have kept the High A–Low A structure at 30–30, but the shift has yet to materialize.

With the addition of Lexington and Lakewood, the Sally League joined the National and the Pacific Coast as the largest leagues of any classification in the United States. A sort of leveling off came in the minor leagues, and many clubs and many leagues stabilized, after these changes to both franchises and classification.

"John Moss never stops," said Ron McKee. "He can work out any problem."

Chapter 20
THE AGE OF TECHNOLOGY

John Henry Moss has done amazing things for the minor leagues. He is the most persistent league president in America, and his longevity with the South Atlantic League stretches beyond that of all other league presidents, including the majors.

The minor leagues have made tremendous progress since the new classification system went into effect in 1963. The minors are in the process of patterning themselves after the major leagues, streamlining ballparks, developing wise marketing procedures, and whipping front office attitudes toward the game into shape.

The days of simply opening the gates and counting the people coming in are history. The minor leagues go out after clientele, attracting people to their parks with good baseball, good promotions, and comfortable seating in a classy setting.

Luxury sky boxes are appearing in new minor league parks. Concessions are upgraded beyond the hot-dog-and-Coke days. Full meals are served in ballpark restaurants, and ample parking provided to get fans up close, within a minute's walk to the nearest gate.

Before long, John Moss said, scoreboards will work by digital imaging, which, Moss believes, will "get some of the paint off the walls"—meaning, of course, the advertising signs on the outfield fences. And clubs are beginning to find national sponsorships, which mean enough money in the coffers to draw more people into the stands. This isn't just a gimmick to build attendance for club revenue, it is directed at giving fans their money's worth and drawing new fans to share in the good times.

Larger, more noticeable All-Star Games are planned, especially in the SAL. "When we had the Sally League All-Star Game in Lakewood, New Jersey," Moss said, "it was quite a show. That operation has a good ballpark with a big digital board, about the same thing they have in major league stadiums.

"There is an area around the outfield, just beyond the fence, where they can seat 2,000 Little Leaguers. That will be a great promotion. Those little fellows will all be future fans coming to the ballpark.

"The space for the Little Leaguers is a picnic area between the outfield fence and a huge bank that goes around the outfield. You can drive a car around the top of this bank, and along the road up there are six huge, steel structures with four signboards to each structure for advertising purposes. There are twenty-four signs from which the ball club gets $15,000 each in advertising revenue. That's $360,000 a year.

Moss presented such ideas as televising the All-Star Game to other Sally League clubs in an effort to upgrade to a higher level of operation and a whole new dimension to the league. He said, "These are the things we have to do to get other owners thinking they can do the same—and they will! That was Mr. Rickey's philosophy, that if people want something enough to work really hard for it, they can achieve it. He applied that philosophy to both his major league and minor league operations, and it worked."

Moss reached a major advancement with the Atlanta Braves for the 2003 season. "They're good people," he said, "and they have built a minor league park in Rome, Georgia, within spitting distance of Atlanta. Rome is about a third the size of Macon, but it's twenty miles nearer Atlanta than Macon and in good drawing distance of that sprawling metropolitan area. In its first season in 2003, Rome drew 246,718 fans, fifth best in the league. Macon's largest attendance ever was 129,723 in 1997.

"This is not new reasoning, placing minor league franchises in or near major league cities," Moss added. "There was a minor league team in Brooklyn, New York, in 2001 that drew great guns."

From top to bottom, the South Atlantic League shows a wide variance in population, but population does not reflect actual drawing power. For instance, Salisbury, Maryland, with a population of only 21,200, draws from the entire Delmarva Peninsula and the Washington, D.C., market area; Asheville (70,000) draws from a 250,000-plus population in Buncombe County and that of all other Western North Carolina counties; Kannapolis (36,700) is within easy reach of the Charlotte metropolitan area; Lakewood (29,800) lies between the marketing area of Philadelphia and Newark; and Hickory (31,200) is in a high-density furniture manufacturing area.

"Demographics of entire areas change rapidly," Moss said, "and in addition, I think the inspiring thing about our industry is that history records that in each generation, new people come into baseball with a fresh approach to enhancing the economic and, actually, the whole development of our game.

"That is happening today, right in front of our very eyes, and is the reason that some teams in leagues like the South Atlantic and the Midwest put a lot of people in their parks. Today's athletes are stronger than those of yesteryear. Some individual players today employ their own fitness instructors to keep them in top physical condition, which helps prevent injury or incapacitation that might interfere with the huge salaries Major League Baseball pays today. That's a new development in the game, and it's one of the best."

Considering the high price of baseball players today, how much more does it cost to operate a minor league team now as opposed to 1959 when John Moss came back into the game as president of the Western Carolina League?

"I remember Fleming Talman, the office equipment man who was president of the board of Community Baseball, Inc., which operated the Asheville Tourists in the 1950s," Moss said. "He was a good man, a sound baseball man, but he had to run the Asheville operation with both hands close to the vest, watching pennies, if I may be allowed an exaggeration. I have clubs in the SAL today paying $200,000 a year for stadium rent, plus maintenance. What would Mr. Talman think? He'd probably drop dead on the spot.

"That's a reflection of the times and of what it takes to operate a minor league team now. If I had told somebody in our league during the 1960s that I expected them to run an operation with a hundred employees, they would have answered, 'Sometimes we don't draw that many fans.'"

But in some of those minor league hills, there is gold! John Moss brought Larry Schmittou into the Sally League in the 1970s to operate the Greensboro franchise. He had been coaching the Vanderbilt University baseball team, making in the range of $15,000 a year, but he sought a position that carried higher salary potential. Schmittou began promoting people like Conway Twitty, the Oak Ridge Boys, Dottie West, and other entertainers of that caliber, and his promo nights at the ballpark attracted thousands of fans.

"When Larry began observing our game," Moss said, "he concluded that we had to have people in the ballpark, and they often needed an incentive beyond baseball to draw them in.

"He was a first-class promoter and turned out to be a good baseball man," Moss added. "He stayed in Greensboro and was so successful that he probably made several million dollars through his operation there. He was a knowledgeable promoter, who concentrated his efforts on good entertainment and selling the idea of coming out to watch the ball club. In doing so, he increased attendance many times and uplifted the entire operation."

Then along came Peter Kirk and a Maryland baseball firm that developed a database and a marketing base in the Washington market. The Delmarva Shorebirds in the SAL was one of three minor league

National Association President Phillip Piton (left) is pictured with John Henry Moss in 1970. Piton served as National Association president from 1964 to 1971.

teams they owned—the others were Bowie, Maryland, in the Eastern League, and Frederick, Maryland, in the Carolina League.

"Peter and his directors" Moss explained, "built those three clubs to the point that they're now drawing about 1,075,000 people a year. They developed sound ways of marketing T-shirts, caps, and jackets, things like that, and they've done it so well that the Washington Wizards of the National Basketball Association use their services.

"That paid for equipment, training, staff, and other expenditures, and the teams turned good profits," Moss added. "Five or six years ago, I started putting together a poor boy's system of demographics in a database. Kirk and the others took that information and brought in consultants and turned it into something almost like computer inventory for a national sales company or a national manufacturing firm. Then they used it to build a whopping business based on their three baseball teams, and eventually they sold the whole thing for almost $36 million to Comcast Spectacore.

"That's what we're doing here, trying to get something like that going on a league-wide basis. Some of the people are still old-timers who are a little hard to bring into an operation like this, but we're getting there.

"There are a lot of kids coming into public and community relations, and they do a whale of a job with a baseball club. They send dispatches and e-mails on last night's games and what their club is doing. Kids are coming out of journalism schools and into our business and they've got a lot of drive, but one thing they don't know a lot about yet is mass distribution. Something like that requires a lot of work, but I've always been a hard worker, and we're getting there.

" The one area we'll be short in," John continued, "is television, but we will have to cross that bridge when we come to it. With so much television emphasis on the major leagues, about the best the Sally League teams could hope for would be some local television."

Back to the ultra-modification of league franchises, Moss said, "It takes time to get teams to venture into accelerated growth. You're better off if you can have someone set an example. That's the way I work. I wedge things along.

"One thing in our favor," he continued, "is that we have some pretty wealthy owners, one who is worth a billion dollars and another whose worth is around $350 million. People like that, though, are so busy with what they already have, with what brought them this far, that baseball is a side venture, and I spend a lot of time with them trying to convince them to modernize their operations.

"I think Lexington and Lakewood are the two best experiences I've had in being able to launch these modernizations in a short period of time. They will serve as catalysts for others. When someone sees someone else succeed with new ideas, he begins to think he can succeed too." Greenville, Charleston West, and Eastlake have followed these.

With a population of 29,800, Lakewood is not a sizeable town. It is a resort area with perhaps a million people living within thirty-five or forty miles. Its location is ideal, about sixty miles southeast of Philadelphia in a strong market area.

Asheville's McCormick Field is the league's smallest stadium. Perhaps 4,000 could be seated there if they were shoe-horned in. It will take more time to get franchises like Asheville to take on John Henry's modernization plans, but each year the Asheville Tourists draw about two times the population of the city, so the club is well run and promotion-minded.

"To accomplish the things I want to accomplish," John Moss said, "I had to go to the places I thought could get it done more quickly, so the first city I worked these things in was Greensboro. I wanted to work this in Columbia also, but that city had dropped out of the league, lacking adequate facilities.

"My approach will be to energize citizens to want something, and when city fathers own the ballpark, it takes public energization to bring things around."

Energizing the public is nothing new to Moss. He used that approach many times when he sat in his office as mayor of Kings Mountain, filling so many local committees with citizens that he always had a good base of operations.

"When I worked with Detroit in the early fifties," he said, "I learned a lot about this business. I never had to worry about dollars. I would always put together a good advisory board that would help me reach Old Joe out there and get him coming to the ballpark. I didn't have to bust my butt on things that others could do better, so I could turn my efforts toward more imminent things. I never had a baseball club that I didn't increase its attendance and revenue—or, perhaps I should say that I never had a club that lost attendance and revenue.

"I never worried about winning an election," he said. "I could always tell pretty much where I was, and at times I had as many as 335 people working on committees in Kings Mountain. I always thought that each of those 335 could influence another ten people among his friends and neighbors, and that would be 3,350 on my side to help me sell my programs. Especially when I went for bond issues, I would try to get people involved."

Chapter 21
A MATTER OF THE MIND

"Let me tell you what I really believe," John Moss said. "I think in a few years we may have the best league in baseball—including the major leagues. We have mid-sized cities or demographic areas that are on the verge of crashing through into big-time operations.

"I call my South Atlantic League entertainment project an alliance," John said. "I use that word, trying to have each city commit to doing a certain number of things besides baseball.

"It's hard to get some of our league's wealthiest people to commit venture money, if you will, for the minor league ball club. If I said to some of them, 'I want you to put on five concerts at the ballpark,' I probably wouldn't get it. So I have to feed them like babies, just a spoonful at a time.

"An exception is the Charleston, South Carolina, club," he said. "Charleston South is a full-grown operation. It's the sort that fits that old saw, the rich get richer. There are a number of ways to get into this mode, and once they get into it, two things happen: (1) they get very excited, and (2) they go out really hustling. It is hard to keep from getting lazy when the edge wears off, but those who stick with it profit by it immensely."

The major leagues pump a lot of money into SAL clubs. They pay all salaries of players, managers, coaches, and trainers. "I do not keep track of this," John Moss said, "because it is the major league teams' responsibility. I would assume that the top salaries of our managers would be in the $45,000 range, and each club has two coaches, who are probably paid $30,000 to $35,000 a year. I suppose the trainers would make $25,000 a year, and in some instances that's for six or seven months of work."

Since the major leagues control player salaries, the South Atlantic League no longer has a salary limit. "Players earn from $1,500 to $1,800 a month," Moss said. "In addition to that, some of our players draw big monthly checks from signing bonuses. All salaries are paid for a full year, and they're on the payroll all year. Some players get long vacations through the off-season, others play in the instructional leagues, and then the first thing they know, it's March and spring training time again.

"The minor league club is responsible for meals and hotel bills. In 2001, the South Atlantic League players got twenty-five dollars a day meal money, and sometimes the parent major league club would pay for another meal each day. The major league club would contact the local club and say they want to give their players an extra meal every day. Major league clubs have dieticians, and one of their responsibilities is to check on what their minor leaguers are eating. The local club may get this extra meal catered, if they wish, snacks and such in the dressing room after batting practice.

"Minor league clubs now have training rooms in which players have the equipment to work out and keep the edge on their physical conditions. The cost is divided equally between major and minor league teams. Coaches keep check on who is using training equipment and who isn't. They want all their ballplayers, major and minor leaguers alike, to keep physically trim.

"These things are life-lasting. Kids learn enough about physical conditioning to keep in shape for life. Trainers attend specialized

John Henry Moss (far left) attends Game 4 of the 1981 World Series in Los Angeles with members of baseball's high brass. Moss sits with National Association President Johnny Johnson along with Baseball Commissioner Bowie Kuhn and Kuhn's wife, Luisa.

schools and have the latest equipment to work with. They leave nothing to chance.

"I watched a young player in Columbia go through all these exercises. He twisted and turned his body, perhaps treating a back pain or something like that, and I couldn't help but think, he's learning something about his body and how to care for it for the remainder of his life. This is a great thing for these youngsters.

"There is no longer any such thing as hand-me-down uniforms from major league teams to their minor leaguers. All Sally League uniforms are new, and the local clubs buy their own uniforms, getting three sets every other year. One thing we liked was to get those large, expensive big league warmup jackets.

"Our league office works out deals with sporting goods companies and our teams usually buy two sets of uniforms and get the third set free. That's a 33 percent savings, which most clubs can use.

"The majors pay for 75 percent of balls and bats, and the minor league club pays the rent and operating expenses.

"You know," John Henry concluded, "the darnedest thing has evolved over the last few years. There are more than a dozen different bat companies now, all turning out pretty good products. It used to be that everybody wanted to use Hillerich and Bradsby's Louisville Slugger, but now a lot of players have their bats custom made by other companies. Some of these companies are very small and are willing to tailor bats to the player's requirements. Some bats are now made of maple instead of ash."

Chapter 22
WORKING FOR THE FUTURE

Back in 1948 when John Moss got the Western Carolina League off the ground and onto its feet, it was a huge success. In that first season of its existence, the league played to a total of 383,380 paying customers, a good Class D attendance for that era and decidedly more than most of the country's Class D leagues. Professional baseball was new and fresh in the WCL's small North Carolina towns, and folks came to the games in droves and brought friends and neighbors with them.

They did it without a lot of hoopla. Clubs promoted ladies nights, Civitan nights, baseball clowns, and one-man softball teams to entertain the crowds, but the major attraction was baseball. People came to see them *play*. Baseball was enough. Whip-armed pitchers and beefy sluggers and speed merchants on the bases were what people wanted. Baseball was a rawboned, muscle-stretching, slam-bang sport that attracted people on its own.

And then something huge happened. Television became widespread. It brought Joe DiMaggio, Stan the Man, Ted Williams, and the Mantle kid from Oklahoma into living rooms all over the country, and the combination of major league baseball and the magic of those eight-inch, round, silver screens pulled fans out of minor league ballparks and plopped them firmly in their favorite easy chairs to watch major league baseball. Before long, home air conditioning added to the appeal of sitting in front of a television set on a hot summer day.

Proliferation came next. On some Saturday afternoons, baseball fans had a choice of two major league games with the voices of Red Barber and Mel Allen, or Tony Kubek, even Joe Garagiola, who talked a better game than he had played, to add color to the game and to our lives.

The minor leagues went into a nose-dive and hit the ground in many cities that were once known as good baseball towns. Major league teams scrambled, seeking greener pastures over the hill or on the West Coast, and new cities came in to widen the scope of the majors, and the game on that level suddenly wasn't what it used to be. Double-A caliber players found places in the major leagues, and many aficionados said the game was watered down.

But it was never watered down in the minors, because those players knew they had to hustle their best if they ever intended to play in the major leagues. That helped increase the caliber of Major League Baseball again. Somewhere along the line someone remembered Bill Veeck bringing the midget, Eddie Gaedel, in to bat in a 1951 St. Louis Browns game. Gaedel is registered in *The Baseball Encyclopedia* as "BR TL 3'7" 65 lbs." He created such a stir in baseball that everybody began looking for midgets.

Clubs began to promote prodigiously, and the minor leagues found it attractive. Good promoters drew good crowds. Men were sought who knew exactly how to pepper baseball with just enough extracurricular activities to make the fans love it. The word got around. Baseball still prevailed as *the* attraction, and the Clown Prince of Baseball Max Patkin put additional people in the stands.

Through its century of service, the South Atlantic League has sent many thousands of players to the major leagues. A few have been granted places in the National Baseball Hall of Fame in Cooperstown, New York. Those giants are listed in the Appendix on page 175.

As feeder teams for the major leagues, the minors and their fans took great pride in following the progress of former hometown players through the major leagues. For example, Asheville watched famed Tourist slugger Willie Stargell climb all the way from the South Atlantic League to the National Baseball Hall of Fame in Cooperstown, New York. Later, Eddie Murray ran the same route—Asheville to Cooperstown.

One further ironic twist added to the rebirth of the minor leagues: The major leagues' nonsensical attitude toward payment of players—with some taking home a bagful of millions every season—that the majors found themselves jacking prices out of the common man's pocket, apparently forgetting that it was he whose support had made the game great. Skyrocketing ticket prices and spiraling concessions costs have taken their toll on the number of major league games a hard-working mechanic can take his family to, and suddenly minor league baseball begun to look better and better with each passing summer.

John Henry Moss has been in baseball a long, long time and has always been an idea man who was open to new means of promotion. He has seen the game change dramatically since his first affiliation in 1948. Technology is the word today; that's where change is coming next.

"When we think of Class A clubs drawing 175,000 to 225,000 people," he said, "and some exceeding 400,000, it shows how much interest there is in minor league baseball, or maybe just baseball, no matter what level. In the old days, a Class D club could survive on about 65,000 fans and do very well. That's only a drop in the bucket to the numbers we're looking for now. In our league, we are hoping that in a few years our minimum club attendance will be somewhere around 250,000 to 275,000, and we expect three or four of our best-drawing clubs to surmount 500,000 attendance. I realize that's a giant step, but it is not out of reach, and, as the old man says, we ain't seen nothing yet."

John explained that the optimum market objective of Sally League clubs is to have facilities that provide revenue streams. By that he means twenty or twenty-two sky boxes, along with club seats, and that each park will have an open-all-year restaurant, and many additional amenities for those who love to see baseball on the flesh.

"We will have to market aggressively," he said, "with 20,000 database marketing capability for each club, along with a radio network with a minimum of four stations, and the televising of games with a minimum of one television station in our market area. This is where we will have to be this century to operate successful Class A Minor League Baseball clubs."

It is no secret that John Moss is an ultra-optimist. If he hadn't been, the WCL would have died a hard death during those difficult times in the early 1960s.

"I think I have always had progressive ideas," John said. "Somewhere along the line, working in the Detroit minor league system in the early 1950s, I began to recognize that if you had the basic population and an attractive product and worked the product well that you could get people out for sporting events.

"A couple of decades ago, Detroit was probably the best sports town in America," John continued. "It had all the major sports franchises, including professional boxing and wrestling, and all of them drew remarkably well. Early in my days with Detroit, I began to observe that sports there had a very sound economic base and both corporate and fan support, and I think that was the basis of my mental makeup that helped me realize that the things I am advocating for the SAL can be done."

Moss agreed that the high cost of Major League Baseball may have put some fans back in minor league ballparks, especially in those parks that are near major league stadiums, like the one in Rome, Georgia, near Atlanta. The true baseball lover who cannot afford the cost of Major League Baseball might go see it twice or three times a year, and if he truly loved the game he would frequent minor league parks. Moss believes the minors are doing a good job of providing affordable, wholesome, exciting family entertainment.

"Each succeeding generation," he continued, "becomes creatures of habit. The child begins to watch television and by the time he becomes a teenager or young adult, he finds himself addicted to it. So, we in the Sally League have come along and tried to provide good fresh-air entertainment with some interaction. And that's a word we're basing a lot of our baseball future on—interaction."

Baseball fans should remember that word.

"Let me explain," John said. "Our next step is to develop something that will have our fans engaging in a contest atmosphere in which they become contestants in the activity on the field. I mean, in the baseball game. This is still somewhere in the future, and is the objective of only a few of the league teams.

"We are going to have big video boards, and in some of our parks we're talking about certain seating sections where fans can compete with each other by pushing buttons on a small board at their seats to contest or agree with a manager's decisions, or a catcher's call of pitches as the game is being played. We will be at that point in a very few years."

This will be advanced entertainment that will put fans directly into the game. Some may call it "Baseball Plus" or, as the league will call it, "Interactive Participation," meaning there will be more for a person to do at the ballpark than watch the game. It will actually put the fan into the game.

He will match wits with the manager and find how well he could manage a team. From his seat, the fan can put his own baseball knowledge to a test by calling for a sacrifice bunt, a stolen base, a hit and run, a steal of home, a pitchout. He will also be able to call the pitches—fastball, curve, slider, changeup, whatever. His opinion will not be registered in the dugout for the manager to see. It will only be a game in which he will match wits with those of other fans in his seating section.

Foremost, the results of his play will show him how much true baseball knowledge he has, and if he outscores the others playing the game, he will win a prize.

"This is a new era in Minor League Baseball," John said. "We will have to use all of our technology to get to the point I'm striving for. To prove how much new technology will help attendance, one saw in 2003 that our top four teams in total attendance were Lakewood, Lexington, Lake County, and Charleston, South Carolina, all of whom had new ballparks with all of the amenities except the contest boards.

"So, those four clubs have reached all of our goals except the contest boards, and they are just beginning to explore the new technology that's out there and is ours to be had. Lexington has definite plans to explore some interactive participation with its fans.

"For the last two seasons, Delmarva has been selecting a contestant by browsing the stands to pick out that fellow over there with the glasses on, or the big guy there who looks like he can throw a baseball a mile and a half, and have them try to throw a baseball into an open convertible from some distance away. Whoever throws the ball into the automobile wins it. We don't draw tickets any more, none of that old-fashioned stuff. This is the way it will be done in the New Era: One fan will be selected each night and he shows up on the screen on the big scoreboard so fans can see him close up and applaud his effort. I'm sure the league teams will come up with other attractive ideas like that.

"So," he concluded this little spiel, "everything creates some additional activity at the ballpark. Obviously, there are a lot of other features we can put in as time goes on that will evolve for those occupying seats in our ballparks.

"Some of our ideas have been tailored to fit baseball activity from the ideas of others. For example, I don't play the video games in hotel rooms, but they're there, and a lot of people choose those hotels because their kids can while away a lot of time. When we get to the ballpark, all of us are kids. We will be even more so when we get a chance to outwit the managers."

One who overheard this conversation with John Henry Moss asked if contest boards was something the major leagues could use. "Yeah," he answered, "but don't tell anybody!"

"Our primary reasons for existence," John Henry said, "are to provide good, clean entertainment for the people of our cities and surrounding areas, and to develop players for the major league teams that work with our clubs. I feel we have been more than successful in both instances. All you need do to ascertain how good the entertainment we provide is to look at the attendance figures of our league. They keep increasing every year.

"To see how well we fulfill our commitment to the majors, let's take a look at the Asheville club, which is typical of all of them in this respect. In the major league playoffs last year (2007), there were eighteen former Asheville Tourists on the roster of the Colorado Rockies, the Tourists' parent club, two more with Cleveland, and one each with the Yankees, the Dodgers, and the Arizona Diamondbacks. That's a lot of talent to come through one city in a short period of time."

Chapter 23
A GREAT LEAGUE—WITH WHISKERS

The South Atlantic League has seen more than a hundred seasons go by since its inception in 1904, and in most of those seasons, the league played an active schedule. There have been three times when SAL play was suspended for up to five years, twice because of world wars and once for the Great Depression. The league missed just the 1918 season because of the First World War. It had played seventy-seven games in 1917 before shutting down for the duration.

The Depression forced a five-season stoppage that included the seasons of 1931 through 1935. Then it played seven more years until the Second World War broke out in 1941, and the league halted play again after the 1942 season, resuming in 1946 after missing three seasons.

There was another time, later on, when the South Atlantic League shut down from 1964 through 1979, but those years were saved when the Western Carolinas League, under the astute guidance of John Henry Moss, assumed the name of the South Atlantic League for the 1980 season and incorporated all of the WCL records for those years into the Sally League record book.

That record book contains hundreds of noteworthy stories, of which only a sampling will be recounted here. The very beginning is the best place to start.

Ty Cobb and the South Atlantic League began their rookie seasons together. The first games in the Sally League were played on April 26, 1904, and Cobb, then just seventeen, made his debut with Augusta against the Columbia team. Cobb hit a double and a home run in that game, getting off to a great start, but the next day he walked into the Augusta business office and drew his release.

Two days later, on April 29, he signed a contract to play with Anniston, Alabama, in the Southeastern League, which wasn't even a member of Organized Baseball. It was called an outlaw league, but it had the thing that attracted Ty Cobb's full attention—a salary of fifty dollars a month!

However, the following season—1905—Cobb showed up again on the Augusta roster. He led the league that summer with a .326 batting average, and at the end of the South Atlantic season he joined the Detroit Tigers and played the last forty-one games there, batting .240. Never again in his playing career, which lasted twenty-four years, through 1928, did he ever bat under .320. He hit over .400 three times and finished with a .367 lifetime average, highest ever recorded in the major leagues.

☆

Second to Cobb on the all-time best hitters list is Rogers Hornsby, second baseman for the St. Louis Cardinals in the National League. Hornsby, like Cobb, batted over .400 three times and finished his twenty-three-year career with a .358 average.

☆

Third place on that all-time hitting list belongs to another who cut his teeth on South Atlantic League baseballs, Shoeless Joe Jackson. Jackson registered a .356 lifetime major league average for three teams during his thirteen seasons. Joe's career came to an abrupt and bitter end in 1920 when he was suspended from Organized Baseball for life in the infamous Black Sox Scandal. When the axe fell, Shoeless Joe was thirty-one, in the prime of his baseball life, and one can only wonder what numbers he would have posted in the last half of a long career.

☆

Gambling, which always keeps baseball on its toes, has been discovered occasionally among Sally League players and even managers. It was handled with as severe a penalty as in the major leagues. On August 11, 1946, Hooper Triplett, a twenty-seven-year-old Columbus outfielder, brother of Coaker Triplett, who played with the Cardinals and Phillies, was fined $500 and suspended indefinitely for betting $20 on a Columbus game. Triplett had won the Sally League batting championship in 1940 with a .369 average. He was batting .314 at the time of his suspension.

Baseball, especially during its early days, had its share of violence in the heat of competition. Some infamous players also were involved in violence off the field, when young blood ran hot and led to incidents of viciousness.

☆

One such case was that of John C. Bender, an outfielder for the Columbia, South Carolina, team. On July 19, 1908, Bender, brother of Hall of Fame pitcher Charles A. (Chief) Bender, was arrested by police and suspended by his team for stabbing his manager, William (Win) Clark, on board a steamer between Jacksonville and Charleston. Bender was reinstated by Organized Baseball for the 1909 season. Two years later, on September 25, 1911, he died unexpectedly of heart failure while pitching a game for Edmonton, Alberta, Canada. He had begun that season with Charleston, South Carolina, in the Sally League but had been released. His body was buried in Charleston.

☆

Another early example occurred on July 5, 1911. Horace Bealey, a catcher for Columbus, was shot and killed in a cathouse in the red-light district of Huntsville, Alabama, during a quarrel with a woman.

☆

Greenville manager Stanley (Frenchy) Bordagaray, a veteran of eleven seasons in the major leagues before taking the reins at Greenville, was fined fifty dollars and suspended sixty days for assaulting an umpire in July 1947. Soon thereafter, he was succeeded as manager by former Cardinals star Johnny (Pepper) Martin, an Oklahoman known as the Wild Horse of the Osage.

☆

On June 21, 1984, nineteen-year-old Saul Lopez, a right-handed pitcher for Macon, was arrested for the murder of a woman who lived in an apartment beside his.

☆

Deep South violence was threatened in Sally League towns during the racial crises of the 1960s, and on one occasion was averted in Savannah in August of 1962 by moving the team's home games to Lynchburg, Virginia, for the remainder of the season.

☆

In contrast to man's acts of violence, nature's violence was in evidence on May 24, 1955, when a concrete outer wall at Jennings Stadium in Augusta collapsed in a strong windstorm. Two boys and a man were killed when the wall fell outward. The incident happened in the fifth inning of a game with Montgomery, Alabama.

☆

When the Charleston, West Virginia, Wheelers returned to baseball in 1986 after a three-year absence, but they missed playing their home opener because of a deep snowstorm.

☆

On September 28, 1989, Hurricane Hugo, one of the most devastating storms ever to hit the southern United States, tore apart College Park in Charleston, South Carolina, home of the Charleston Rainbows. Federal disaster funds and a $600,000 insurance policy gave Charleston the means to rebuild the ballpark before the start of the 1990 season.

Automobile accidents have also taken their toll on the Sally League.

On September 6, 1925, Augusta manager Emil Kuhn and outfielder Frank Reiger were killed in an accident when their car overturned on a curve near Camden, South Carolina. The wreck injured five other team members riding in the car, none seriously. Kuhn was killed instantly and Reiger died soon after.

☆

Twenty-two-year-old SAL umpire Mark Connors was killed in an automobile accident in Asheville on July 11, 1981.

Those who have watched Sally League games down through the years have seen unusual, and even spectacular, plays and games, such as those that follow.

☆

Charlie Morgan, Macon catcher, recorded his twelfth straight hit on June 24, 1925.

☆

The Asheville Tourists won the SAL pennant in 1928 with a team so good that the commissioner of baseball himself, Kenesaw Mountain Landis, conducted an investigation into the sale of six players directly to the major leagues at the end of the season, thinking the club was possibly breaking up a great team simply for money. Landis looked into the records of the team and was satisfied that the deals were legitimate. The Tourists had sold outfielders Ben Chapman and Dusty Cooke and pitchers Joe Heving and Joe Marty to the Yankees. Pitcher Bill Harris was purchased by the Pittsburgh Pirates and pitcher Harry Smythe by the Philadelphia Phillies.

Harris led the team with a 25–9 record and Smythe was 16–11. Heving was 13–5 and Marty 1–1. Heving's 2.46 ERA led the league. Spectacular figures also showed up for Chapman and Cooke. The Asheville team hit 60 home runs, 240 doubles, and 112 triples and finished with a team batting average of .304 and 109 stolen bases. It won ninety-seven games and lost forty-seven, beating out Macon by eighteen games for the pennant. Chapman played fifteen years in the majors, ending with a lifetime .302 batting average, and then managed the Philadelphia Phillies from 1945 to1948. When he was fired during the 1948 season, he was replaced by his former teammate, Dusty Cooke.

☆

Charlotte southpaw Jim Mooney put on quite a show on the evening of July 19, 1930. Hurling in the Sally League's very first night game under lights, Mooney struck out twenty-three batters in a nine-inning contest against Augusta. Charlotte won, 7–3.

☆

April 23, 1946, was a day of destiny for second baseman Eddie Kazak in Columbus, Georgia. He broke into the Columbus lineup that day, and in his first game, belted two home runs in Columbus's eight-run eighth inning. He also had a single and double in five at-bats and stole home. Eddie was called to the major leagues by the St. Louis Cardinals in 1948 and batted .273 for five seasons. What made Eddie's case so interesting was that he was severely wounded in the invasion of Normandy in 1944 and spent sixteen months in a veterans hospital before his discharge in October of 1945.

☆

Something most unusual happened in Columbus on April 24, 1954. A twenty-one-year-old man from Detroit named Joe Carolan arrived early and bought a ticket to get into the game. He asked for a tryout as an outfielder with the Columbus club and hit the ball so well in batting practice that he was signed to a contract an hour before the game began. Put in the Cardinals' lineup to start the game, Carolan came up with the bases loaded in the bottom of the first inning and hit a grand slam home run in his first at-bat as a professional player. He never reached the majors, however.

☆

On April 17, 1956, Juan Pizaro, a $35,000 bonus baby from Puerto Rico, made his professional debut with Jacksonville and struck out fourteen batters in a six-inning stint. Four days later, on April 21, he fanned twenty-one and allowed four hits and one walk in a twelve-inning 1–0 victory over Charlotte. He won twenty-three games that season and struck out 318 to lead the league in both categories. Only two years before, Pizaro had been a batboy in the Puerto Rican League. He went up with the Milwaukee Braves the following season and pitched in the thrilling 1956 and 1957 World Series against the Yankees. His major league career lasted eighteen seasons.

☆

Ron Rozman, pitching for the Augusta Tigers, lost to Charlotte 3–0 after winning fourteen consecutive games on August 31, 1957. He finished 15–1 with a league-leading 1.64 ERA.

☆

Asheville's 1961 team sent eight players through Pittsburgh's pipeline to the major leagues, including Hall of Famer Willie Stargell. Pittsburgh sent a stream of pitchers through Asheville early in the season, and manager Ray Hathaway's Tourists began to put distance between themselves and the rest of the league.

A pitcher named Jim Hardison arrived in Asheville from Class C Kinston in mid-May. He knew that Asheville's lineup was loaded with sluggers, and when he arrived at the Asheville airport, he told general manager Jim Mills, "I may not lose a game this summer." By mid-July he was 11–0, then he lost one, but he ran his string to 15–1 in late August and wound up 18–2 with a 2.75 ERA.

☆

In 1976, Paul Mirabella led the league with 136 strikeouts, LaRue Washington with 106 runs, and Harold Kelly with 13 wins and a 3.02 ERA. All of these played for the Tourists.

☆

Vince Coleman, playing for Macon in 1983, was the fastest runner many baseball fans had ever seen. Coleman could run like a deer and sometimes appeared to be only a streak heading toward second. He hit .350 that summer and stole 145 bases, an all-time minor league record. Vince went up with the St. Louis Cardinals two years later (1985) and stole his major league high of 110 bases in his rookie year. In eleven seasons, Vince stole 752 2/3 bases, sixth on the all-time list, and led the National League in thefts his first six seasons.

There were a few pitching streaks that should be remembered.

☆

In 1959, when Asheville returned to baseball after a three-year hiatus, the Tourists opened the season with a rag-tag team of has-beens and others who were cut from various minor league training camps. One was an aging player named Harry Fisher, who pitched in the Pacific Coast League in the early 1950s. Fisher, whose arm was considered to be gone, tried to play the outfield for the Tourists, but on a Sunday afternoon, after a tough Saturday night on the town, Fisher staggered under a blazing sun and managed to miss four easy fly balls in right field.

General manager Art Perkins released Fisher that evening, and before Fisher could leave town the next day, manager Clyde McCullough telephoned from Charleston and said one of his relievers had a sore arm and couldn't throw. "If Fisher's still in town," McCullough said, "re-sign him and get him down here quick."

Perkins located Fisher, signed him to a new contract—at a raise in salary, on Fisher's demand—and dispatched him to Charleston by Trailways. Fisher answered that challenge by pitching twenty-three consecutive innings of hitless ball in relief over the next two-and-a-half weeks.

☆

In 1984, Henry Carson, pitching for Savannah, threw 39 $^{2}/_{3}$ consecutive shutout innings. That's the equivalent of four-plus consecutive shutout games, followed by a 12 $^{2}/_{3}$-inning shutout.

Without question, baseball is a fickle game.

☆

On September 4, 1916, a Macon pitcher named Bellars threw a no-hitter against Columbus in the opening game of a doubleheader. But how things turned around in the second game! Columbus's bats came alive and pounded out twenty-six hits in a 14–11 victory.

☆

Columbia, which posted a 100–54 won/lost record in 1952, became the first SAL team ever to win a hundred games. No one has won that many since. To show how fickle the game can be, Augusta lost twenty-one consecutive games that year, the most in South Atlantic League history, breaking its streak with a 6–1 victory over Jacksonville on June 6. Greenville, which lost sixteen straight in 1928, held the record previously. Indeed, the game is one of wins and losses.

☆

In 1960, Savannah manager Ray Hathaway had Donn Clendenon, a tall young man from the Caribbean, playing left field, which ended against a fence about six feet high. An Asheville hitter belted a long fly ball that would have dropped over the fence for a home run had the lanky Clendenon not climbed the fence, stood atop it, stretched his six-foot-four frame upward, and caught the ball as it went out of the park.

Asheville manager Charlie Kress screamed like a banshee, belabored the umpires for calling the ball a home run, and finally posted a hundred-dollar protest fee, claiming Clendenon was out of the playing field when he caught the ball. However, the league's protest committee ruled against Kress because the rule book stipulates that the fence is part of the playing field so Kress and the Tourists lost the hundred dollars and the game.

Ironically, that Savannah team, manager and all, was moved

by its parent Pittsburgh Pirates to Asheville the following season. Asheville won the Sally League pennant by thirteen games, and eight of its players were promoted to Pittsburgh in the next two years. Old-time fans call that team possibly the greatest in the long history of baseball in Asheville, which had a professional baseball as early as 1897.

Looking back over the years, John Moss said, "We've had excitement of both kinds, natural and manufactured, in the South Atlantic League for many years, and judging by the league's growth in recent years, we're due to have more excitement in the years to come."

Chapter 24

NO LONGER CRANKING THE WHEEL—BUT STILL AROUND

The time always comes for good men to retire. John Henry Moss was well past the normal retirement age, but still going strong. The league had blossomed and grown during the half century of his life that he had devoted to it.

"That's when I began to think of retirement," he said, "when I realized that my fifty years at the wheel would soon be up. Few people keep the same job for a half-century, and very frankly, we had been tied down rather much to community life because of our obligations in the mayor's office combined with our work in baseball."

John Henry's use of *our* included his wife, Elaine. She had been by his side for forty-five years, serving as administrative assistant of the SAL, which, along with her regular job as controller of J. E. Herndon Company, a cotton waste firm in Kings Mountain, kept her as busy as her ever-working husband. Elaine passed away June 19, 2004, and lies resting in the Moss plot of Mountain Rest Cemetery in Kings Mountain.

If ever two people put almost all of their time into operating a baseball league, John Henry and Elaine Moss did—and the league profited hugely by their efforts. They maintained the league office in their home, where they often entertained the leading dignitaries of the baseball world. Branch Rickey had eaten at their table. So had Gen. William Westmoreland, who commanded the American army through the Vietnam War, and several secretaries of the army and navy, governors, senators, and dignitaries from many fields.

The Mosses could see the results of the work they had done, raising the South Atlantic League into the largest baseball circuit in the nation at sixteen teams. All around them were the improvements and additions to Kings Mountain that had come about during John Henry's twenty-four years in the mayor's office.

"When I thought of fifty years rolling around on the league's work, and how far the league is strung out," John Henry said, "I began to think it would be kind of nice to relax in old age. I thought I had taken the league far, and I realized that the operation of the league will go on after I am no longer cranking the wheel."

His successor is Eric Krupa, who has been living in Tampa, working for the National Association of Minor League Baseball. "Eric is a bright man," John said. "He has been in league finance for ten years. He spent a week with me during our playoffs in 2007. We went to West Virginia and saw some games and had two workdays together here in the office. I think he will do a great job as league president, and he will continue to breathe fire into the league, as I have done for half a century."

Even though he stepped down from the league president's office at noon on January 1, 2008, John Henry Moss isn't absent from league duties. He has been voted to the office of president emeritus, and his contract in that position reads the way it did in his presidency—for life.

John Henry Moss is flanked by National Association President Mike Moore (left) and Jimmie Lee Solomon, the executive vice president of Operations for Major League Baseball. Moore served as National Association president from 1992 to 2007.

"I will use that position cooperatively," he said, "without embarrassing anybody or trying to run out in front."

He set the hour of his retirement at noon on New Year's Day for a reason. "That," he said, "permitted me to serve as president of the South Atlantic League under eight different presidents of the National Association of Minor League Baseball." He listed them as George Trautman, Phil Piton, Hank Peters, Bobby Bragan, Johnny Johnson, Sal Artiaga, Mike Moore, and the new president, Pat O'Conner.

Things have happened on ball fields that made league presidents pull their hair out. John Henry was no exception. He encountered sticky problems in both his first and last years as president of the WCL/SAL.

One evening in his first year, John Henry attended a game in which one of the teams was managed by George Wilson. Jack Hiatt, who batted right-handed and also threw right, was catching, and in arguing a strike call with umpire Devoil Butcher, he was thrown out of the game.

John Henry was in attendance that evening, and George came to him and said, "Mr. President, I'm out of ballplayers." He had been substituting, and when Hiatt was thrown out it created a dilemma.

"Well, grab the mitt," John Henry said. "You're not too old to catch a little."

George protested, "But, John, I'm left-handed."

"Then get the first base glove," John said.

"We don't have a left-handed one of those, either," George said.

"Get back in the dugout," John Henry said. "I'll be over in a minute." He sat there thinking what he was going to do.

He walked to the dugout and asked, "Where's Hiatt?" He was on the other end of the bench, and John Henry called him over.

"Hiatt," he said, "I'm fining you fifty dollars, putting you back in the ball game, and the fine is to be paid before you leave the ballpark."

With the score tied near the end of the game, Hiatt walked, took second on a fly to the outfield, and Aaron Pointer drove him home to win the game.

"Both of those guys are in the South Atlantic League Baseball

Hall of Fame," John Henry said. "Pointer was inducted in 2006 and Hiatt in 2007.

"By the way," he added, "Pointer that year batted .402, which still stands as the league record. He later officiated in the National Football League for fifteen years and is now evaluator of officials for the NFL."

The toughest problem John Henry faced in his fifty years as league president came on the final weekend of John's final season, 2007.

Kannapolis and Greensboro played their final series of the season against each other in Greensboro. The series began on Thursday night and the teams got into a shouting, pushing, shoving match. The umpires threw ten men from each team out of the game.

John, in Kings Mountain, was having dinner in a restaurant. When he arrived home, his telephone was ringing, and he was presented with the problem of the brawl. Neither team had enough eligible players to finish the game.

"Anybody in the stands?" John Henry asked.

"Yes," he was told, "6,500 and some."

"Then the game will be finished," John said. "Put the players back in and I will take care of this misconduct after I read your report. I will make a decision on this before tomorrow."

As fate would have it, John Henry was scheduled to be in Greensboro for the game the following night, Friday. Nine thousand people were in the stands, some hoping to see another fracas. They were not disappointed.

In that game, an incident occurred—and the benches cleared, and another pushing and shoving match erupted on the field. The umpires ejected ten more from each team, leaving both teams short of players.

John Henry came onto the field, huddled with the umpires, and told them, "We're going to finish this game. I want your reports written up tonight and get them to me in the morning."

So John worked on the problem all day Saturday, went back to Greensboro that evening, reinstated the players in order to play the game that night, and fined all of them again. "Real investigating was required to determine who were the leaders of that brawl,"

John said, "but we got them sorted out and I suspended six players into the 2008 season and levied fines on twenty-two men from each club."

The teams played on Sunday and closed the season on Monday, Labor Day. Meanwhile, both events were monitored by the parent major league clubs of the two teams involved, and several players were reassigned to other teams before the playoffs began following Labor Day.

"The whole thing," John Henry said, "was the fact that two teams got together and being young people, as they are, they expressed themselves.

"That, however," he said, "is a part of the game. I will say that in this league, everything has gone all right for the last decade— with the exception of that last fracas. Things like that happened,

Former major league manager and Texas League icon Bobby Bragan, brother of SAL President Jimmy Bragan, shares a moment with John Henry Moss. Bragan also served as president of the National Association from 1976 to 1978.

and they're going to happen in every league, and they have to be handled quickly. The incidents in Greensboro were started by a hit batsman on Thursday night and a hard slide into second base on Friday night."

Both John Henry and his late wife, Elaine, are in the South Atlantic League Baseball Hall of Fame, he as president who has taken the league to its farthest reaches and she as one of the best administrative assistants he could have hired.

"When I had to be gone, visiting the cities in the league," he said, "if a problem arose in the office, she handled it as well as I would have done. I always thought we made a good team. When Ron McKee was president of the Asheville baseball club, he used to say, 'Well, she runs the league, anyway.'

"It wasn't only in baseball that she helped me so much, but in my position of mayor. She was highly respected by the citizens of Kings Mountain, and she was a great hostess at the public functions we held. She was a very outstanding lady."

And he, to make a long story shorter, was an outstanding man who knew baseball as well as any person, and who operated the Western Carolina League and the South Atlantic League through a long and successful half century.

Appendix

NOTEWORTHY PERSONALITIES OF THE SAL—SOME FACTS AND STATS

The South Atlantic League in recent years has been filled with future big-league stalwarts. Many outstanding current major leaguers who were developed by the Sally League are: Bobby Abreu, Jeff Baker, Clint Barmes, Derek Bell, Craig Biggio, Barry Bonds, Pat Borders, David Cone, Aaron Cook, Manuel Corpas, Cliff Floyd, Jeff Francis, Brian Fuentes, Rafael Furcal, Ron Gant, Marcus Giles, Luis Gonzales, Vladimir Guerrero, Brad Hawpe, Todd Helton, Matt Holliday, Chris Iannetta, Derek Jeter, Ubaldo Jimenez, Andruw Jones, David Justice, Joe Koshansky, Kenny Lofton, Fred McGriff, Franklin Morales, Juan Morillo, Andy Pettitte, Juan Pierre, Mariano Rivera, Ivan Rodriguez, Scott Rolen, Jeff Salazar, Reggie Sanders, Curt Schilling, Kevin Seitzer, Sammy Sosa, Ryan Speier, Ryan Spilborghs, Ian Stewart, Cory Sullivan, Quilvio Veras, David Wells, Jake Westbrook, and Mark Wohlers.

Among the many Sally Leaguers who went on to manage in the big leagues are Willie Randolph and Cecil Cooper. At least a dozen former Sally League umpires work on major league playing fields today.

The roster of Sally League graduates reads like a *Who's Who in Baseball.* Listed alphabetically, here are some of the SAL's noteworthy people and some of their accomplishments:

HENRY (HANK) AARON hit .362 with 22 HR, 115 runs scored, and 125 RBI for Jacksonville in 1953. Jacksonville won the pennant by two and a half games over Columbia and drew 142,721 fans, about 35,000 more than any other team. In his professional career, he played for Atlanta and both the American and National Milwaukee teams. Aaron was baseball's all-time HR leader (755) and all-time

RBI king with 2,297. Barry Bonds (son of Bobby Bonds) broke the HR record in the 2007 season. Aaron was a two-time batting champion, four-time HR king, and four-time RBI champion in the major leagues. He was inducted into the National Baseball Hall of Fame in 1982.

JOHNNY ALLEN of the Asheville Tourists struck out 137 batters to lead the league in 1929. He had a good big league record of 142–75 with the Yankees, Indians, Browns, Dodgers, and Giants.

WALTER (SMOKEY) ALSTON played first base for the SAL championship Columbus team in 1939. He ended that season by playing the last sixty games without an error. He managed the Dodgers for twenty-three years, leading the Brooklyn franchise to its only World Series in 1955, and to a pennant in 1956 before the Dodgers moved to Los Angeles. In L.A., his clubs won world titles in 1959, 1963, and 1965 and pennants in 1966 and 1974. The Dodgers finished in first place in the division nineteen times in Alston's twenty-three years, winning 2,040 games in regular season play.

GEORGE (SPARKY) ANDERSON managed the Rock Hill Cardinals in the WCL in 1965 before leading the Asheville Tourists to the Southern League title in 1966. In 1970, he replaced Dave Bristol as manager of the Cincinnati Reds. He guided the Big Red Machine teams to five pennants and four World Series in nine years. The Reds won World Series championships in 1975 and 1976. Then in 1979, Sparky took the reins of the Detroit Tigers and managed them to two pennants and one successful World Series before retiring in 1995 after his 26th year as a major league manager. He was the first manager from the SAL to reach the big leagues and was inducted into the National Baseball Hall of Fame in 2000.

LEONARD (LEN) BARKER III, a hard-throwing righthander, helped guide the Gastonia Rangers to the WCL championship in 1974. He won 11 decisions in twenty games while allowing only 101 hits in 124 innings, and striking out 140 batters. He posted a solid 3.34 ERA with Gastonia. In his first major league start with the Texas Rangers on October 3, 1976, he pitched a three-hitter against the Chicago White Sox. He won nineteen games and led the American

League in strikeouts with the Cleveland Indians in 1980. On May 15, 1981, he reached one of the greatest achievements in Major League Baseball by pitching a perfect game against Toronto. He led the league in strikeouts (181) and started the All-Star Game for the American League in 1982. He won seventy-four games in eleven major league seasons.

JAMES (JIM) BAYENS had a long and successful career as a baseball executive and scout. Bayens operated three clubs in the SAL. He was general manager at Shelby in 1981, Gastonia in 1982, and Savannah from 1987 to 1990, leading that team to two SAL championships. Bayens became traveling secretary for the St. Louis Cardinals in 1971 and was promoted to director of scouting and player development in 1975. He scouted for the Cardinals again from 1991 to 1995.

DONALD (DON) BEAVER has applied a huge amount of knowledge and business acumen to both major and minor league baseball, with much success. A native of Statesville, North Carolina, he purchased the Gastonia Rangers and relocated them to Hickory, changing the name to the Crawdads. The team became an instant phenomenon. Their nickname has become one of the most popular merchandising logos in sports and has been featured in national publications like *The Sporting News, Rolling Stone,* and *Baseball America.* He has owned the Crawdads, who won the 2002 SAL championship, during their sixteen years of existence. From this experience, Don has expanded his efforts to include current or previous ownership interest in the Pittsburgh Pirates, Charlotte Knights, New Orleans Zephyrs, Tennessee Smokies, and the Winston-Salem Warthogs. He currently serves on the SAL executive committee and board of directors.

DAVID (BUDDY) BELL played for the Sumter Indians in the WCL in 1970, where he batted .265 with 117 hits, 19 doubles, 3 triples, 12 HR, and was named to the All-Star Team. He joined the Cleveland Indians in 1972 as an outfielder and was selected for the Rookie All-Star Team by *Baseball Digest, The Sporting News,* and Topps. He moved to third base, and won six straight Gold Gloves from 1979 to1984 with the Texas Rangers. He also won the Silver Slugger Award in 1984. Buddy was a five-time Major League Baseball

All-Star selection (1973, 1980, 1981, 1982, and 1984). During his eighteen-year major league career, he also played for Cincinnati and Houston.

SHELDON (CHIEF) BENDER had a distinguished baseball career that spanned more than six decades. He managed the Columbus Cardinals in the SAL in 1952–1953 and then oversaw development of Cincinnati's Big Red Machine as head of minor league operations for the Reds from 1967 to 1989. The National Association named him King of Baseball in 1996, and he served as senior advisor for player development for the Reds. The Reds' Minor League Player of the Year Award is named for Chief Bender.

BILL BETHEA, a left-handed pitcher, had an outstanding season with Lexington in the WCL/SAL in 1960. His 1.35 ERA led the league and remains the SAL record today. Bethea also holds the league record for most strikeouts in an extra-inning game (25) and most strikeouts in two consecutive games (41). He played six years in the minors in the Toronto organization.

BILL BLACKWELL began his baseball career on radio for the Springfield (Illinois) Redbirds in 1978 and became vice president/general manager of the Columbia Mets of the SAL. He was a three-time winner of the SAL Executive of the Year Award. In 1987, he became vice president/general manager of the Jackson (Mississippi) Generals of the Texas League, serving thirteen years in that capacity, and won his fourth Executive of the Year Award when he was in the Texas League. From 2000 through the 2002 season he was president and general manager of the Greensboro Bats of the SAL. He later became vice president and general manager of the Charlotte Knights before becoming assistant general manager of the Richmond Braves in 2006.

WINSTON BLENCKSTONE purchased the Florence Blue Jays of the SAL and owned them from 1987 through the 1992 season. He moved the franchise to Myrtle Beach, where the team won the SAL championship twice. Blenckstone moved the franchise again, to its present home in Hagerstown, Maryland. The team is the Hagerstown Suns. Blenckstone served as vice president of the SAL, chairman of the

SAL executive committee, and was the SAL representative to the Board of Trustees of Minor League Baseball.

BOBBY BONDS played with the Lexington Giants in 1965 and scored a WCL-leading 103 runs. He was chosen as the WCL's Most Outstanding Prospect that year. During a fourteen-year career, he played for eight different major league clubs and cracked the 30-HR, 30-stolen-base plateau five times (a record matched only by his son Barry). His debut in the majors came in 1968 with the San Francisco Giants, and he slugged a grand slam HR in his third big-league at-bat. He was a three-time All-Star (1971, 1973, 1975) and a Gold Glove winner in 1971, 1973, and 1974. Bonds was the Major League Baseball MVP in 1973 and holds the major league home-run record with 332.

BOB BONIFAY was the general manager of a record six SAL teams (Augusta, Columbia, Jacksonville, Knoxville, Macon, and Montgomery). After a highly successful baseball career, Bonifay retired from the Macon baseball club in 1968 to become executive director of the Georgia section of the Professional Golf Association.

LAWRENCE (LARRY) BOWA played for Spartanburg of the WCL in 1966 and still holds the WCL/SAL records for highest won-lost percentage for a championship team (.722) and most consecutive wins in a season (25). He finished 5th in batting for Spartanburg in his first professional season.

Bowa set the WCL record for fielding percentage by a shortstop (.972) and consecutive errorless games streak for a shortstop (26). He played twenty years professionally, including sixteen in the major leagues with the Phillies, Cubs, and Mets. He was the starting shortstop for the Philadelphia Phillies, hitting .375 in the 1980 World Series and starting a World Series record seven double plays. Larry has managed two major league clubs—the San Diego Padres and the Philadelphia Phillies. He was named 2001 National League Manager of the Year for guiding the Philadelphia Phillies to their first winning season since 1993. In 2007, he was hired by the Dodgers and is currently their third-base coach.

HARLEY BOWERS was a longtime Georgia sports writer and former editor of the *Macon Telegraph,* covering Minor League Baseball in Albany and Macon. He was instrumental in spearheading the effort to renovate Luther Williams Field and return SAL baseball to Macon in 1991. In 1986, he was named Sports Columnist of the Year by the Sportswriters Association and has been twice named Georgia Sports Writer of the Year for the National Sportscasters and Sportswriters Association.

JAMES (JIMMY) BRAGAN hit .308 for the Columbia Reds in 1955. Bragan also played second base for Savannah and Macon in the SAL. He was a scout for Cincinnati from 1958 to 1966 and a longtime major league coach for the Reds, Expos, Brewers, and other teams before becoming president of the Southern League, a position he held for fourteen years. Bragan is also a member the Alabama Sports Hall of Fame and was King of Baseball in 1994.

LELAND (LOU) BRISSIE was a left-handed pitcher who played for Savannah in 1946 and 1947. On nights when Brissie pitched, crowds numbered 6,000 to 11,000, often with fans seated on the grass in the outfield. A World War II hero, Brissie was badly injured in Italy in 1944. He pitched with a leg brace and posted a 25–5 record in 1947. He led the league with 278 strikeouts and a1.91 ERA. Brissie went on to pitch in the major leagues for the Philadelphia A's and the Cleveland Indians. He won fourteen games in 1948 and sixteen games in 1949 for the A's. Brissie played seven years in the major leagues and later served as national director of American Legion Baseball. Brissie's number 3 was retired by the Sand Gnats in 2008—a first for the team.

JAMES (DAVE) BRISTOL was a native of Macon, Georgia, who managed the Macon team in 1962 and 1963, winning 161 games in those two seasons. Living in Andrews, North Carolina, he became the only Tar Heel to manage four major league teams in an eleven-year managerial career—Cincinnati, Atlanta, Milwaukee, and San Francisco. In addition to managing, he serves as third-base coach for the Reds, the Expos, the Braves, the Giants, and the Phillies.

JAMES (KEVIN) BROWN was a right-handed pitcher for Columbia and led the SAL with 221 strikeouts and a 2.74 ERA in 1983. He made his Major League Baseball debut in 1986 with the Texas Rangers, then played for Baltimore (1995), Florida (1996–1997), and San Diego (1998). In 1998, he signed the richest contract in baseball history to date with the Los Angeles Dodgers. He finished his career with the Yankees (2004–2005). He was a six-time All-Star and a World Series champion.

WILT BROWNING covered the Greenville Spinners for the *Greenville (SC) News* and the Charlotte Hornets for the *Charlotte Observer.* He served as sports editor and columnist for the *Greensboro News* and the *Greensboro Record* where he played a role in the SAL's return to the old Greensboro Memorial Stadium. Wilt also served as sports editor and columnist for *The Asheville Citizen-Times,* covering the Tourists in the Sally League. He covered the Atlanta Braves for the first six years the team was in Atlanta before serving as executive sports editor of the *Atlanta Journal.* He worked seven years as public relations director for the Atlanta Falcons and Baltimore Colts in the National Football League. Wilt was a five-time North Carolina Sportswriter of the Year and is the author of several books.

DICK BUTLER served as SAL president in 1953 and 1954 as part of a baseball career spanning forty-nine years. He served in both major and minor league executive positions. His career also included stints as assistant to Baseball Commissioner Happy Chandler; as president of the Texas League from 1955 to 1963; and supervisor of umpires for sixteen years under American League presidents Joe Cronin, Lee MacPhail, and Dr. Bobby Brown.

STEVEN (STEVE) CARLTON pitched a 10–1 season with a 1.03 ERA for Rock Hill in 1964. He was a strapping six-foot-four, two-hundred-pound left-hander who recorded 329 major league victories in a twenty-four-year career. He made his debut with Cardinals in 1965 and soon blazed to prominence, winning 14, 13, 17, 10, and finally 20 for the Cardinals through 1971. He was traded to Philadelphia in 1972 and played there until 1986. He also pitched for the Giants, White Sox, Indians, and Twins before retiring in 1988 with a record of 1,833 walks and 4,136 strikeouts. He participated in five league championship series, ten All-Star Games, and four World Series (two with the Cards and two with the Phillies) and received four Cy Young Awards. Carlton was inducted into the National Baseball Hall of Fame in 1994.

ALBERT (HAPPY) CHANDLER, SR., succeeded Kenesaw Mountain Landis as commissioner of baseball and held the office from 1945 until 1951. He wore many hats throughout his life, including service as a United States Senator from Kentucky in 1939 through 1945 and governor of Kentucky from 1935 to 1939 and again from 1955 to1959. Happy played an integral role in SAL history by encouraging and supporting the reorganization of the league and its designation as a Class A league in 1945, following the league's suspended operations during World War II. He had the foresight to take care of major league players after their careers were over by creating the baseball pension fund. He also instituted the assignment of six umpires to World Series games. In 1982, Chandler received baseball's highest honor, induction into the National Baseball Hall of Fame.

TYRUS (TY) COBB played in the SAL's first game in 1904. He started in center field for Augusta in the league's inaugural game. Just seventeen years old, Cobb homered and doubled in that game. He hit .305 to lead the SAL in 1905. Cobb became a baseball legend in Detroit, where he played from 1905 to 1926. He then played for the Philadelphia Athletics from 1927 to 1928. His .367 career batting average is still the highest on record. Cobb was inducted into the National Baseball Hall of Fame in 1936, one of the five inaugural members.

DREW COBLE was a true student of the game of baseball whose umpiring career began in 1975 in the WCL. In his first year in the league, he called the league's All-Star Game. He spent another year umpiring in the WCL before working his way up to the major leagues. Starting as an American League umpire in 1982, he again worked his way toward a goal and attained it in 1991, when he became an umpiring crew chief. Drew played a part in many of the game's finest moments. He served on crews of six American League championship series, plus three division series, two All-Star Games, and the classic World Series between the Atlanta Braves and Minnesota Twins. He retired from umpiring in 1999.

VINCENT (VINCE) COLEMAN, destined to terrorize National League pitching with base stealing, playing for Macon in 1983, when he set the all-time minor league record with 145 stolen bases. He was selected to the SAL All-Star Team, and was voted the league's most outstanding Major League Prospect. He went on to win the National League Rookie of the Year Award in 1985 with the Cardinals, leading the National League in stolen bases from 1985 to 1990. He ranks 6th all-time in stolen bases (752), and holds Major League Baseball's longest streak of stolen bases without being thrown out (50). Coleman also played for the Mets, Royals, Mariners, Reds, and Tigers before retiring in 1997.

MURRAY COOK played for Gastonia in 1963–1964 where he was an All-Star shortstop before becoming the team's general manager in 1965 and 1966. Farm and scouting director for the Pittsburgh Pirates occupied his time from 1975 through 1982, and then he worked the 1983 and 1984 seasons as general manager of the New York Yankees. He later served as general manager of the Montreal Expos and vice president and general manager of the Cincinnati Reds.

JOHN (WES) COVINGTON, a Jacksonville outfielder, led the SAL with a .326 average, in 1955. The following year he debuted with the Milwaukee Braves and played in two great World Series against the Yankees, in 1957 and 1958, when he hit 24 HR. The Braves won in 1957 and lost in 1958. He played for six major league teams and is one of only a few players to have played for four different teams in one season (1961). He retired in 1966.

CECIL DARBY was a longtime sports writer and editor for more than 30 years of the *Columbus (GA) Ledger-Enquirer*. Darby began his baseball career as the clubhouse man and bus driver for the Columbus baseball team. Darby is a well-known writer who is relied upon by many ball clubs and journalists for Sally League and Southeastern baseball history. Darby was instrumental in the creation of the Chattahoochee Valley Sports Hall of Fame.

VAUGHAN (BING) DEVINE worked as the business manager for the Columbus Cardinals in the SAL in 1946-47, when the club drew the two largest attendance totals in the city's history. He was promoted to work in St. Louis the following year, became the assistant general manager of the St. Louis Cardinals in 1955 and was promoted to general manager in 1957. He is credited with building four World Series teams with the Cardinals (1964, 1967, 1968) and Mets (1969) over his eighteen-year career as a general manager. Devine was also the president of the NFL St. Louis Cardinals.

ARTHUR (RED) DWYER had a long and distinguished career as both a player and an executive. Dwyer posted a record of 8–4 for Macon in 1946. He pitched for Rock Hill in 1947 and later owned and operated the franchise in the Class B Tri-State League from 1948 to 1951. He was also general manager of the Charlotte Hornets in the Southern League from 1970 to 1972.

JACK FARNSWORTH was one of the mainstay owners during the lean years of the WCL and helped carry the WCL and the SAL into the illustrious regard that it enjoys in the baseball world today. From 1978 to 1988, he was owner-operator of the Gastonia club, and he also served as vice president of the WCL/SAL. During his time as vice president, he served as chairman of the league's finance committee, where he assisted in developing markets for clubs to relocate.

JULIAN FINE was active in Savannah baseball for more than fifty years. Judge Fine was known throughout the Savannah area as Mr. Baseball. When times were bleak for baseball in Savannah, Judge Fine spent his personal time, money, and efforts to convince the major league clubs to come to town.

CURTIS FLOOD, playing for Savannah, scored 98 runs to lead the league in 1957. He began his career with Cincinnati but played most of his year with the St. Louis Cardinals at center field. He was a three-time All-Star, two-time world champion (1964, 1967) and a seven-time Gold Glove winner. Flood may be best remembered for his challenge of the reserve clause in contracts.

ROBERT (DOUG) FLYNN served the SAL as both a player and coach. He coached the Capital City Bombers, in Columbia, South Carolina, during the 1996 season, helping his team gain a berth in the playoffs. That season he was honored as Coach of the Year in the New York Mets organization. Flynn played on one of the greatest baseball teams in history as a member of the Cincinnati Reds' famed Big Red Machine. His timely hitting and late-inning defensive work helped the Reds capture back-to-back world championships in 1975 and 1976. During his eleven seasons in the majors, Doug played for the Reds, Mets, Texas Rangers, Montreal Expos, and Detroit Tigers. Flynn's other accomplishments include tying the record of three triples in a game in 1979, ranking in the Top 10 all-time for fielding percentage at second base, and winning a Gold Glove in 1980. He managed the Gulf Coast Mets to a league title in 1997.

PACK (BOB) GIBSON was a fearless, fireballing pitcher who played for Columbus in 1957. He became a star with the St. Louis Cardinals, winning 251 games in seventeen seasons, and posted a 7–2 mark in three World Series, of which they won two. Gibson had a lifetime 2.91 ERA and posted an incredible 1.12 ERA in 1968, winning twenty-two games. His #45 was retired by the Cardinals. He was a eight-time All-Star, a nine-time Gold Glove winner, and two-time Cy Young Award winner. He was inducted into the National Baseball Hall of Fame in 1981.

THOMAS (TOM) GLAVINE of the Sumter Braves led the SAL in 1985 with a 2.35 ERA, a portent of things to come. A left-handed pitcher, Glavine played for the Atlanta Braves, then the New York Mets, before returning to Atlanta to again play for the Braves. He was a ten-time All-Star, two-time Cy Young Award winner, and a 1995 World Series champion.

MARVIN GOLDKLANG and his Goldklang Group are the principal owners of six minor league clubs across the country, including the Charleston RiverDogs of the SAL. Goldklang is a Wall Street lawyer, and his experience around the business of sports is extensive. His clubs have won every conceivable operations award given to professional sports operators.

JOHN (GORDO) GORDON began his broadcasting career in 1965 as the voice of the Spartanburg Phillies. After five years with Spartanburg, Gordon joined the Baltimore Orioles where he remained until 1973. He accepted the broadcasting job at the University of Virginia, becoming the voice of Cavaliers football and basketball. Gordon joined the Yankees' Class AAA affiliate Columbus Clippers in 1977 and worked five years there before becoming part of the New York Yankees broadcast crew in 1982. In 1987 he moved to the Minnesota Twins as radio analyst, a job he currently holds. John and his family devote countless hours and effort in support of the Fellowship of Christian Athletes.

LEON (GOOSE) GOSLIN, an outfielder from New Jersey, led the Sally League in hitting for Columbia in 1921 with a .390 average, 124 runs, 214 hits, and 131 RBI. Goslin became a legend in the majors, playing for the Washington Senators, the St. Louis Browns, and the Detroit Tigers. In 1928, he led the American League in hitting with .379. Goslin played eighteen years in the majors (1921–1938) and posted a lifetime batting average of .316. He played in five World Series, hitting 7 HR. He ranks 10th on the World Series HR list. He was inducted into the National Baseball Hall of Fame in 1968.

ROBERT (BOB) HAGER was the first broadcaster of the WCL's Lexington Giants. Over thirty-five years, he told stories the whole world heard. He was called by former NBC Nightly News anchor Tom Brokaw "our Cal Ripken of correspondents." As a general assignment reporter for NBC, his coverage of the news was worldwide, from the Vietnam War to political unrest in Panama. Hager helped set the standard for making coverage of stories which ordinary lives were touched by, such as hurricanes and airline disasters. He retired from NBC News in November of 2004.

DUDLEY (MIKE) HARGROVE, first baseman for Gastonia, led the league with a .351 average in 1973. He had twelve good seasons with Texas, San Diego, and Cleveland, hitting above .300 five times. He was the American League Rookie of the Year in 1974 and an All-Star in 1975, then went on to manage the Cleveland Indians, the Baltimore Orioles, and the Seattle Mariners.

CHARLES (CHARLIE) HARVILLE, a longtime radio and television personality, began his career covering sports in 1938, broadcasting the baseball games of the Thomasville Tommies. He did the radiocasts for the Greensboro Patriots from 1949 through 1952, and then covered High Point/Thomasville in the WCL and its offspring, the new SAL. Charlie covered the current Greensboro franchise's return to the SAL. He worked fifteen years on the Atlantic Coast Conference's football and basketball networks and has covered wrestling and NASCAR from its humble beginnings to its widespread popularity of today.

DANNY HAYLING was born in Costa Rica and made history in 1960 while playing for the Hickory Rebels by pitching twenty-four complete games and winning twenty-two. He won his first seventeen starts before suffering his first professional loss. Although he pitched until 1967, Hayling did not advance past Class A in the United States; he spent eight seasons in the Mexican League.

JACK E. HIATT, a steady defensive outfielder/first baseman, with the Los Angeles Angels' organization in the WCL in 1961. He played for the Statesville Owls and helped lead them to the league playoffs. His batting average was .325 with 108 hits, including 20 doubles, 4 triples, 3 HR, and 69 RBI in ninety-six games. Jack spent nine seasons in the major leagues (1964–1972), splitting his time between the L.A. and the California Angels, then the Giants, Expos, Cubs, and Astros. He was the Giants' director of player development for sixteen years until his retirement in 2007.

MARCUS HOLLAND was the scorekeeper of record for nearly all of Savannah's Southern League professional baseball games from 1968 to1983. In addition, Marcus spent more than fifty years as a copy boy, sports reporter, sports editor, and editor with the *Savannah Morning News* and *Savannah Union Press*. As a reporter in the 1950s and 1960s, he covered the Savannah Indians, Redlegs, Parrots, and White Sox, all of the old SAL. In August 2004, the Savannah Sand Gnats named the press box at historic Grayson Stadium in honor of Marcus for his many contributions to the prosperity of baseball in Savannah.

ED HOLTZ, late general manager of the Macon Braves, had a distinguished career as a baseball executive, serving as general manager for several minor league clubs, including Appleton, Wisconsin, and Chattanooga, Tennessee.

LEO HUGHES co-owned two pro baseball teams with R. E. Littlejohn in Spartanburg for nineteen years. He was co-owner of the Spartanburg Peaches of the Tri-State League from 1946 through 1955, helped bring baseball back to Spartanburg in 1963 as a member of the WCL, and co-owned the franchise through 1971. He received the prestigious Larry MacPhail Award for promotion and won two straight WCL championships in 1966 and 1967. The team that he and R. E. Littlejohn owned together led the WCL in attendance five times.

BROOK JACOBY, of Anderson, led the SAL with 108 RBI in 1980. He made his major league debut in 1981 playing part of 1981 and 1983 for the Atlanta Braves. He went on to play for the Cleveland Indians (1984–1991), then was traded to the Oakland A's where he completed the 1991 season. He finished his playing career in 1992 back in Cleveland. He was a two-time All-Star (1986, 1990) and currently serves as the hitting coach for the Cincinnati Reds.

WILLIAM (BILLY) JOHNSON led the SAL in games played (142) in 1939 for Augusta and played in the inaugural SAL All-Star Game that summer in Columbus. Johnson led the SAL in triples (20) and tied for the lead for games played in a season (150). He had a nine-year major league career with the Yankees and Cardinals. Johnson made his debut with the Yankees in 1943, winning the Baseball Writers Association of America Rookie of the Year Award. He played in two major league All-Star Games and four World Series.

LARRY (CHIPPER) JONES is the third baseman of the Atlanta Braves and is one of the most fearsome sluggers in the National League. Chipper was first overall pick in the 1990 baseball draft and spent his first full professional season in the SAL with the Atlanta Braves Class A farm team, the Macon Braves. In 1991, he blossomed into a future major league Hall of Fame player. He was named an All-Star and the SAL's Most Outstanding Prospect that season, posting a batting average of .326 with 245 total bases, 104 runs (tied with Jason Hardtke), 11 triples, 98 RBI, and 154 hits. He led Macon to the second-half South Division title, and went up to the major leagues with the Braves in 1993. He played a major role in Atlanta's winning the World Series in 1995 and was chosen the National League's MVP in 1999. He was the first active player ever elected to the SAL Hall of Fame.

KEN KAISER was an umpire who logged thirty-three years at all levels of baseball, both major and minor leagues. Ken umpired in the WCL during the thirteen years he spent in the minors. He went on from there to become an American League umpire for twenty-three years. He worked the plate for Gaylord Perry's historic 300th victory on May 6, 1982, and umpired the World Series of 1987 and 1997, the major league All-Star Game in 1991, and officiated in eight major league playoffs. Ken was voted the Most Colorful Umpire in the American League in a 1986 poll by *The Sporting News.*

CHARLES (DOC) KANUPP began officiating baseball and football while still in high school. He had a twenty-year career umpiring in professional baseball and was Senior Official in the Western Carolina League. He served as a mentor to the young umpires with whom he worked, helping them develop skills, and two of them went on to umpire in the major leagues.

HARMON KILLEBREW hit .325 for Charlotte in 1956. He then hit 573 HR in a twenty-two-year major league career with the Washington Senators/Minnesota Twins and a final year with the Kansas City Royals. He was a six-time American League HR champion and three-time RBI king, an eleven-time All-Star, American League MVP in 1969. The Twins retired his #3 in 1974. Killebrew was inducted into the National Baseball Hall of Fame in 1984.

THEODORE (TED) KLUSZEWSKI helped return the Sally League to the diamond after missing three seasons in World War II. In 1946, he hit .325 for Columbia to lead the league. He played eleven years for Cincinnati (1947–1957) and four more for other teams (Pittsburgh Pirates, Chicago White Sox, Los Angeles Angels), in a good major league career. He led the league in most runs in 1949 and 1954 and in RBI in 1954 (141), as well as being a four-time All-Star. The Reds retired his #4 in 1998. Kluszewski remained a hitting coach for the Reds and hitting instructor for their minor league program until his retirement in 1986.

THOMAS (TOMMY) LASORDA pitched for the Greenville Spinners of the SAL in 1949, then played for the Brooklyn Dodgers in 1954 and 1955 and the Kansas City A's in 1956. Lasorda managed the Los Angeles Dodgers for twenty seasons, and during his tenure the Dodgers won 1,599 games, captured eight National League West titles, four National League pennants, and two World Series championships (1981 and 1988). He managed in sixty-one postseason games and four All-Star Games. He was National League Manager of the Year twice and winner of the Branch Rickey Award in 2006. He led the U.S. Olympic team to a gold medal in 2000, which he regards as the greatest moment of his life. The Los Angeles Dodgers retired Lasorda's #2 in 1997, the same year he was inducted into the National Baseball Hall of Fame.

PERRY LIPE, a pitcher, third baseman, and outfielder for Macon, set a minor league record by playing 1,127 consecutive games over a ten-year period for several teams. He snapped his streak when he left the club to go to the bedside of an ill relative on August 26, 1911.

R. E. LITTLEJOHN, well known for his generosity, co-owned two professional baseball teams in Spartanburg with Leo Hughes for nineteen seasons. He co-owned the Tri-State League's Spartanburg Peaches from 1946 through 1955. He helped bring baseball back to Spartanburg in 1963 in the WCL and co-owned the Spartanburg Phillies through the 1971 season. Mr. R. E. led one of the WCL's premier franchises to five attendance titles and won the prestigious Larry MacPhail Award and back-to-back WCL championships in 1966 and 1967.

ALFONSO (AL) LOPEZ hit .326 for Macon in 1928 and caught 114 games. He went up to the Dodgers at the end of the 1928 season. He became a solid major league catcher for nineteen seasons, catching 1,918 games, which stood as a record for forty years. Lopez managed seventeen years in the majors, winning 1,410 games. He managed the 1954 Cleveland Indians who won 111 games. Lopez was inducted into the National Baseball Hall of Fame in 1977.

DWIGHT LOWRY, the late manager of the Fayetteville Generals, had the best record (86–55) in the SAL in 1995. The following year, he led the Generals to a second-half SAL division title and was named the Detroit Tigers Player Development Man of the Year. Lowry was a catcher with the Minnesota Twins and was a member of the 1984 World Champion Tigers team. In 1997, the Detroit Tigers renamed that award to the Dwight Lowry Award in his honor, after Lowry's sudden death at the age of thirty-nine.

LE ROY (ROY) MAJTYKA, former player, major league coach, and veteran minor league manager, ranks in the top twenty of all time for wins by a minor league manager. He managed the Piedmont Phillies in the South Atlantic League.

DONALD (DON) MATTINGLY led the SAL with a .358 average and 177 hits while playing for the Greensboro Hornets in 1980. He played his entire twelve-year career with the New York Yankees and had a lifetime batting average of .307. He was the 1984 American League batting champion (.343), the 1985 RBI king (145), a six-time American League All-Star, a nine-time Gold Glove winner, and Atlantic League1985 MVP. The Yankees retired his #23 in 1997.

RON MCKEE has been a beneficial member of the SAL for two decades, serving as general manager and part owner of the Asheville Tourists since 1980. During his twenty-six years of service in Asheville, McKee was named the SAL's Executive of the Year three times (1984, 1990, and 1996), and under his leadership, *Baseball America* in 1981 named the Tourists the top Class A organization in the country. Ron served as second vice president of the SAL until his retirement in 2004.

CHIP MOORE is the current first vice president and a member of the board of directors of the SAL, and has spend three decades with the Atlanta Braves organization, serving at various times as vice president and controller. He began working with the Braves as an usher at Atlanta-Fulton County Stadium and then spent nine years as a member of the team's grounds crew. He joined the Braves' accounting department in 1985 and by 1992 was their controller. He was involved in the design and construction of stadiums in the Braves minor league organization, including Rome's State Mutual Stadium and Mississippi's Trustmark Park.

CHARLES B. MORROW moved from his native Chicago to fulfil a lifelong dream of owning a baseball team when he purchased the Columbus RedStixx. Morrow was a sports visionary who renovated Golden Park and took baseball to a new level in Columbus, Georgia. He was also instrumental in bringing Cottonmouths hockey to Columbus and creating the Chattahoochee Valley Sports Hall of Fame. Morrow died in 1998.

ELAINE BEILKE MOSS, wife of John Henry Moss, served as director of administration and finance for the WCL/SAL for forty-five years. She operated the league office during the years John served as president until her death in 2004. Elaine was actively involved and personally contributed greatly to the survival and growth of the Western Carolinas League and the continuing growth of the South Atlantic League.

JOHN HENRY MOSS founded the current South Atlantic League in 1960 when it was known as the Western Carolina League. He has the longest tenure of any minor league president and in 1989 was given a lifetime contract by the SAL board of directors. Moss has served as chairman of the Executive Committee of the National Association of Professional Baseball Leagues, Inc., and was the longtime vice chairman of the Council of League Presidents.

DALE MURPHY was six foot four and two hundred pounds in 1975, when he made his debut with Greenwood in the WCL/SAL and was selected for the All-Star Team. He still holds the record for most games played in a season by a catcher (129). He was moved to the outfield in the majors, where he played fifteen years for Atlanta, two years for Philadelphia, and his final year (1993) with the Colorado Rockies. In his big league career, Murphy slugged 398 HR (averaging 28 per season) and making 2,111 hits in 2105 games started. He played in the National League championship series in 1982, and was a seven-time All-Star, five-time Gold Glove winner, and two-time National League MVP. Atlanta retired his #3 in 1994.

EDDIE MURRAY split his second professional season between Miami and Asheville in 1974. He came back to Asheville in 1975 and hit .264 with 17 HR and 68 RBI. Murray debuted in 1977 with the Baltimore Orioles and played there until 1988. He went on to play with L.A. Dodgers (1989–1991), New York Mets (1992–1993), Cleveland Indians (1994–1996), Baltimore Orioles (1996), Anaheim Angels (1997), and the L. A. Dodgers (1997). He was one of only four players with 500 HR and 3,000 hits, joining Hank Aaron, Willie Mays, and Rafael Palmeiro, and he is the all-time RBI (1917) leader among switch-hitters. Murray was an eight-time All-Star, three-time Gold Glove winner, and 1997 American League Rookie of the Year. Baltimore retired his #33 in 1998. Eddie hit 4 HR in three World Series and finished 10th on the career list with 10,603 at-bats. He was enshrined in the National Baseball Hall of Fame in 2003.

PHILIP (PHIL) NIEKRO honed his pitching skills in the SAL, hurling thirty-eight games for Jacksonville, finishing with a 6–4 record and 2.79 ERA. Niekro won 318 major league games, mostly with the Atlanta Braves (1964–1983, 1987). He also pitched for the New York Yankees (1984–1985), Cleveland Indians(1985–1986), and Toronto Blue Jays(1987). Phil had a devastating knuckleball pitch. Twice, Niekro led the National League in victories and in 1969 propelled the Atlanta team to the National League West title, recording a career-high 23 victories, 21 complete games, and a 2.57 ERA. A five-time big league All-Star and five-time Gold Glove winner, Phil pitched a 1973 no-hitter against the San Diego Padres. Phil won 121 games after turning forty, the most wins by anyone in that age category. He led the National League with a 1.87 ERA in 1967, his first season as a starter in Atlanta, and had the National League's best won-lost percentage in 1982 with a 17–4 record for an .810 winning percentage. In 1984, Atlanta retired his #35, and he was enshrined in the National Baseball Hall of Fame in 1997.

OTIS NIXON, playing for Greensboro in 1980 scored the SAL's

most runs (124). He also holds records for stolen bases (67) and walks (113). He debuted with the Yankees in 1983. He also played for Cleveland, Montreal, Atlanta, Boston, Texas, Toronto, Los Angeles, and Minnesota. He is the older brother of Donell Nixon of Bakersfield, who in 1983 stole 144 bases in the California League. Otis Nixon is 16th in the list of all-time base stealers.

DAN O'BRIEN, SR., began his baseball career as general manager of the Burlington, North Carolina, baseball club of the Carolina League in 1955. From 1956 through 1963, he was general manager of the Boise, Idaho, baseball club; of the Jacksonville, Florida, club in the SAL; and of the Greenville, South Carolina team in the WCL. O'Brien served as the assistant to the president of the National Association of Professional Baseball Leagues; vice president and general manager of the Texas Rangers (1973–1978); president of the Seattle Mariners (1980–1983); vice president of baseball administration for the Cleveland Indians (1986–1989); vice president of baseball operations for the California Angels (1992–1993); in baseball operations in the Arizona Fall League; and finally as executive director of USA Baseball.

PAT O'CONNER has been an integral part of Minor League Baseball for two decades. Pat began his career in 1982 as general manager of the Greenwood Pirates in the SAL. The Houston Astros made him their director of Florida operations in 1986, a positiion he held until 1993. He joined the National Association of Minor League Baseball as chief operating officer on May 1, 1993, and was promoted to vice president of administration in December of 1995. Pat also resumed his role as COO in 1998. He worked diligently to help plan, develop, and execute Project 1999, which helped the SAL grow to its current club membership of sixteen. He took office as president and CEO of Minor League Baseball in 2008.

AL (SCOOP)OLIVER was a hard-hitting outfielder/first baseman, who spent his first full professional season (1965) in the WCL. He overcame a serious knee injury and became one of the "Baby Bucs" while with Gastonia, a Pittsburgh farm team. He led the WCL with 159 hits to which he added a .309 batting average, 77 runs, 19 doubles, 5 triples, 10 HR, 13 stolen bases, and 71 RBI. Al played in the majors eighteen seasons, with the Pirates (1968–1977), Rangers (1978–1981), Expos (1982–1983), Giants (1984), Phillies (1984), Dodgers (1984), and Blue Jays (1985). He won the 1982 National League batting title with a .331 average, was a seven-time All-Star and 1971 World Series champion.

MICHAEL C. PATERNO, the late managing partner of the Charleston AlleyCats, loved baseball and was mainly responsible for keeping Minor League Baseball in Charleston, West Virginia. He oversaw the growth of the Charleston ball club and the renovation of Watt Powell Park.

GEORGE PIPGRAS, a pitcher who played with the Charleston, South Carolina, team, led the Sally League with 175 strikeouts in 1922. He began his career with the Yankees the following spring (1924, 1927–1933). He played for the Red Sox from 1933 to 1935, recording a career 102–73 won-lost record, a 4.09 ERA, and was a three-time World Series winner with the Yankees (1927, 1928, 1932). After his playing career ended, Pipgras became an American League umpire, then worked as a scout for the Red Sox.

AARON POINTER was the last man to hit .400 in the minor leagues, posting a .402 batting average with the Salisbury Braves of the WCL in 1961. The league's All-Star first baseman, he also led the circuit with 117 runs, 40 stolen bases, 18 doubles, 14 triples, and 129 hits. He was instrumental in Salisbury's winning the WCL pennant that season. Aaron reached the major leagues with Houston in 1963 and played baseball through 1972, part of the time in Japan. After retiring as a player, Aaron had a distinguished career as a game official in the National Football League. He was a brother of the famous singing group, the Pointer Sisters.

GARY PUTMAN, Greenville pitcher, posted fourteen victories before suffering his first loss in 1966. With this strong pitching, Greenville finished 2nd to Spartanburg, a team that won twenty-five consecutive games in July and August.

PATRICK (PAT) PUTNAM had one of the best seasons in WCL/SAL

history in 1976, playing for Asheville. Pat was the WCL HR king (24), batting champion (.361), and RBI leader (142). He still holds the all-time record for most hits in a season with 194, most RBI, and most intentional walks in a season (15). He was named the Minor League Player of the Year by *The Sporting News*. He played for the Texas Rangers (1977–1982), Seattle Mariners (1983–1984), Minnesota Twins (1984), and the Mariners again (1984).

ARTHUR (BUGS) RAYMOND posted a 35–11 pitching record for Charleston, South Carolina, in 1907. He pitched then for the Cardinals and Giants (1909 through 1911) and lost his life in 1912 at the age of thirty.

H. B. (SPEC) RICHARDSON was a longtime baseball executive and Columbus, Georgia, native who began his career with Columbus in 1946. He went on to become executive vice president and general manager of the Houston Astros and was directly responsible for construction of the Astrodome. Later he became general manager of the San Francisco Giants where he was named Major League Executive of the Year in 1978.

BRANCH RICKEY made his debut in 1905 for the St. Louis Browns and played for them until 1914. He managed the St. Louis Browns and Cardinals and became the general manager of the Cards from 1925 to 1942, the Brooklyn Dodgers from 1943 to1950, and the Pittsburgh Pirates from 1950 to 1955. He led the Cardinals to four World Series championships and one national league pennant with both the Cards and the Dodgers. He was so integral in the formation of the Western Carolinas League (and the eventual rebirth of the South Atlantic League) that this league might never existed without his leadership and financial backing.

One of baseball's most honored men, Mr. Rickey made many memorable contributions to the game, probably not any more important than his signing of Jackie Robinson, who broke baseball's color line in 1947. He did this with full support from then Commissioner Happy Chandler, and the three—Rickey, Chandler, and Robinson—showed great courage through that historic movement. After Rickey's career of playing and managing, he spent half a century in the front office as baseball's most visionary executive. Rickey served as manager or executive of the St. Louis Browns (1913–1915), the St. Louis Cardinals (1917–1942), the Brooklyn Dodgers (1943–1950), and the Pittsburgh Pirates (1950–1959). Minor League Baseball owes a tremendous debt to Rickey for his creation of the modern baseball farm system, which provided player assistance to the minors and promoted new ways of training and developing players for the majors. With the Dodgers Rickey built baseball's first all-encompassing spring training complex in Vero Beach, Florida. He was inducted into the National Baseball Hall of Fame in 1967.

MEL ROBERTS began his twenty-five-year career in 1961 as a player, manager, and coach in the Philadelphia Phillies organization. Roberts managed the Spartanburg Phillies in the SAL from 1988 to 1991. He led Spartanburg to the SAL championship in 1988 and was named an All-Star manager. Roberts served as Philadelphia's first-base coach from 1992 to 1995 and also managed the Atlanta Braves. The late Mel Roberts felt that his greatest achievement had been his commitment and work with young people to help them excel at both baseball and life.

ROBERT (BOB) ROBERTSON led the WCL with 32 HR and 98 RBI, while with Gastonia in 1965, then bested his own record the next year with Asheville. Known for hitting very long distances, he was a three-time minor league home run champion. He played with Pittsburgh (1967, 1969–1976), Seattle (1978), and Toronto (1979). Robertson and Al Oliver were teammates on the 1971 Pittsburgh team that won the World Series, four games to three, over the Baltimore Orioles.

FRANK ROBINSON hit .336 with 25 HR and 110 RBI for the Columbia Reds in 1954 with his 112 runs leading the SAL. Robinson became a major league star, slugging 586 HR in twenty-one big league seasons. He played in five World Series, hitting 6 HR, then became the first African-American manager in major league history when he took over the reins as skipper of the Cleveland Indians in 1975. Robinson was Manager of the Year in 1989, a twelve-time All-Star, and 1956 National League Rookie of the Year. He was inducted into the National Baseball Hall of Fame in 1982.

VERNER ROSS spearheaded the effort to keep professional baseball in Greenville, South Carolina, in 1965 as owner of the Greenville franchise. The Greenville Red Sox won the WCL championship in 1970 and continued to play in the WCL through the 1972 season. Because of a fire at Greenville's Meadowbrook Park, Ross moved the team to Orangeburg for two seasons. His teams consistently ranked among the leaders in the WCL. Ross always displayed great love and passion for baseball, his family, and the Greenville community.

NOLAN RYAN played for Greenville as a nineteen-year-old rookie, striking out nineteen in an 8–0 victory over Statesville. He posted a 17–2 record, striking out 272 in 1966, finishing the season in the majors with the New York Mets. He holds the major league career records for seasons played (27), seasons pitched, strikeouts, and no-hitters, among others. He also holds various major league single-season records for strikeouts. Ryan pitched for the Mets, California Angels, Astros, and Rangers, winning 324 games in his twenty-seven-year major league career. He set all-time records with 5,714 strikeouts and 2,795 walks. He pitched seven no-hitters in the majors and pitched in four league championship series, eight All-Star Games, and was a World Series champion. He retired in 1993, and is the only player to have his number retired by three teams: the Angels #3 in 1992, the Rangers #34 in 1996, and the Astros #34 in 1996. He was inducted into the National Hall of Fame in 1999.

RYNE SANDBERG led the SAL in games played (136) and at-bats (539) with Spartanburg in 1979 and debuted with the Phillies in 1981. He was widely regarded as the best second baseman in baseball while with the Chicago Cubs (1982–1994 and 1996–1997). Sandberg has major league career marks for fielding percentage (.990) and most consecutive errorless games (123) by a second baseman. Sandberg is a ten-time All-Star, was the 1984 National League MVP, and won nine consecutive Gold Gloves from 1983 to 1991. The Cubs retired his #23 in 2005, the same year he was inducted into the National Baseball Hall of Fame.

GENE SAPAKOFF has been the SAL correspondent for the *Charleston Post & Courier* and *Baseball America* since 1987. Sapakoff was instrumental in promoting the building of Joseph P. Riley, Jr. Park (known as The Joe), home of the Charleston RiverDogs.

JOHNNIE SHIVES was a minor league umpire for 19 ½ seasons in the North State, Piedmont, Western Carolina, and Carolina leagues. Shives began working in semi-professional baseball in 1932 for area industrial leagues and worked his first professional game in 1943. He umpired for 30 ½ seasons.

ENOS SLAUGHTER hit .325 for Columbus in 1936 and led the SAL in triples with 20. His aggressive, all-out style became the trademark of the St. Louis Cardinals, for whom he played from 1938 to 1942 and 1946 through 1953. He played for the Yankees in 1954–1955, the Kansas City A's in 1955–1956, then back to the Yankees from 1956 to 1959, finishing his career with the Milwaukee Braves in 1959. Slaughter collected 2,383 hits and a lifetime batting average of .300 in his major league career. He was a ten-time All-S tar and won four World Series championships. St. Louis retired his #9 in 1996. He was inducted into the National Baseball Hall of Fame in 1985.

LONNIE SMITH of Spartanburg led the WCL with 114 runs and 150 hits in 1975. In his seventeen-year career in the majors, he played for Philadelphia (1978–1981), St. Louis (1982–1985), Kansas City (1985–1987), Atlanta (1988–1992), Pittsburgh (1993), and Baltimore (1993–1994). He was a 1982 All-Star, a three-time World Series champion, and was named the National League Comeback Player of the Year in 1989.

PAUL SNYDER was with the Milwaukee/Atlanta Braves organization from the time he signed with them as a player late in 1957 until his retirement in 1963. He managed two clubs for the Braves in the WCL/SAL as a player-manager. Snyder returned to the WCL in 1972 to manage the Greenwood Braves to a 70–61 record, placing 3rd in the eight-team league. The Atlanta Braves promoted Snyder to director of scouting in 1977 and to assistant vice president of scouting in 1983. He then spent 1991 to 1995 as special assistant to the general manager and served as the Braves' director of scouting and player development from 1996 until his retirement in 2007. *Baseball America* named Snyder one of the top twenty-five of the most influential people in baseball.

MARTIN (MARTY) SPRINGSTEAD was a SAL umpire in 1963 and then spent twenty-one years umpiring in the American League (1966–1986). He was an American League crew chief from 1974 to 1985 and worked three All-Star Games (1969, 1975, 1982), four league championship series (1970, 1974, 1977, 1981, 1984), and three World Series (1973, 1978, 1983). Currently, Springstead is executive director of umpiring for the American League, a position he has held since 1986.

DON STAFFORD, a first baseman, won the Spaulding (minor league) Rookie of the Year Award in 1948 and the Hillerich Silver Bat Award in 1952 as the minor leagues' batting champion. Stafford was a four-time All-Star in seven minor league seasons.

WILVER (WILLIE) STARGELL became a member of the Asheville Tourists in 1961. He went on to hit 475 HR in his twenty-one-year major league career and twice led the National League in homers. Willie led the Pittsburgh Pirates to six league championship series and two World Series (1971 and 1979). He was a seven-time All-Star, and in 1979, Stargell was named World Series MVP as well as co-MVP of the National League. He was inducted into the National Baseball Hall of Fame in 1988.

ALAN STEIN currently serves as president and CEO of Lexington Professional Baseball Company and the Lexington Legends. He also works as COO for Ivy Walls Management Company, a national company that owns multiple minor league baseball and other sports teams. He realized a lifelong dream when he brought Minor League Baseball to Central Kentucky and set a baseball standard with completion of Applebee's Park in 2001. His business success with the Legends made him a national leader in the sports industry.

MIKE SZEMPLENSKI was assigned in 1963 by the Boston Red Sox to pitch for Statesville in the WCL. He struck out 313 men and had nineteen games in which he fanned ten or more hitters. The longevity of these records is incredible, considering that major league Hall of Fame strikeout kings such as Nolan Ryan and Steve Carlton pitched in the league after Mike set the records in 1963.

BOB TERRELL began writing for *The Asheville Citizen-Times* in 1949 and spent thirty-seven years full-time for that newspaper. He is now retired, but still writes for the *Citizen-Times* on special assignments. He spent twenty years as sports editor and baseball writer, covering the Asheville Tourists and other teams in the South Atlantic, Tri-State, Southern, and Western Carolina leagues. He has written seventy books in the last thirty years, including a history of Asheville's McCormick Field.

MIKE VEECK is the son of Bill Veeck, longtime owner of the St. Louis Browns, Cleveland Indians, and Chicago White Sox in the American League. As a member of the Goldklang Group, Veeck is part-owner of six Minor League Baseball teams, including the SAL's Charleston RiverDogs. Mike is promoter of the Fun is Good motto that has helped his teams routinely reach attendance and customer service milestones. Mike is founder of the Veeck Promotional Seminar, considered to be the hallmark for marketing and promotional ideas in minor league baseball.

FRED WERBER, from the Augusta Tigers, stole seven bases in a nine-inning game, setting a minor league record on June 11, 1927. That record would be equaled later by Lee Mazzilli and Rickey Henderson.

JOSEPH (JOE) WEST umpired in the Western Carolinas League from 1974 to1976. He also umpired in the Florida Instructional League, Carolina League, Southern League, American Association, and the Puerto Rican League before joining the Major League Baseball umpire staff in 1978. He has worked two major league All-Star Games (1987 and 2005), division series (1995, 2002, 2005), seven league championship series from 1981 to 2004, and the 1992, 1997, and 2005 World Series. A singer/songwriter, he has performed with many country western stars. Born in Asheville, Joe works in both American and National leagues, wearing #22. He is the designer of the West Vest, high-end umpire gear.

HOYT WILHELM was famous for his knuckleball and won seventeen games and had a 2.66 ERA for Jacksonville in 1949. He spent eight years in the minors and three years in military service before breaking into the majors in 1952 at the age of twenty-nine. He was 15–3 for the Giants as a rookie. He pitched in the majors for twenty-one seasons with the Cardinals, Indians, Orioles, White Sox, California Angels, Atlanta Braves, Chicago Cubs, and the L. A. Dodgers. Wilhelm was a five-time All-Star, pitched in 1,070 games, and recorded a lifetime ERA of 2.52 before retiring in 1972 at the age of forty-nine. He was inducted into the National Baseball Hall of Fame in 1985.

EARL WILLIAMS started his playing career in the WCL in Greenwood, South Carolina, in 1969 and led the league in home runs with thirty-three. He spent eight years during th 1970s in the major leagues, playing with the Atlanta and Montreal clubs in the National League and with Oakland and Baltimore in the American League. Williams played a total of 889 games, earned a career batting average of .247 with 756 hits, including 115 doubles, 138 HR, and 457 RBI. In1971, he was the National League Rookie of the Year.

PAT WILLIAMS played baseball in Florida in the minors before becoming the general manager and president of the Spartanburg Phillies. Williams was considered a master of promotion and helped Spartanburg set a team attendance record of 173,010 in 1966, winning the Larry MacPhail Trophy for outstanding promotion. In 1967, Williams won *The Sporting News* Minor League Executive of the Year Award. Also a veteran of the National Basketball Association, Williams served as general manager of the Philadelphia 76ers, Chicago Bulls, Atlanta Hawks, and Orlando Magic. He is the author of numerous books and the father of nineteen children, of which fourteen were adopted.

MATTHEW WINTERS played for the Greensboro Hornets from 1980 to 1982, and he was selected to the SAL All-Star Team all three seasons. In addition, he was named the league's MVP and the Yankees' Minor League Player of the Year in 1982. He went on to play in the Southern League and in the International League in Japan. He made his Major League debut with the Kansas City Royals in 1989. Winters also played for the Nippon Ham Fighters, the club for which he is now an international scout, from 1990 to 1994.

Members of the SAL Baseball Hall of Fame

In 1994, John Henry Moss and the board of directors of the Sally League agreed to establish a South Atlantic League Baseball Hall of Fame that would serve as a regional equivalent to the national hall of fame. The Hall of Fame includes players; umpires and score keepers; front office staff, club owners, and general managers; and baseball writers and newscasters. At the summer All-Star Game in 1994, the first class of eight men was inducted. Currently ninety men and one woman have been enshrined, and everyone included had something to do with the great progress the South Atlantic League has made over the years. Those ninety-one baseball greats are listed here by their year of induction.

Class of 1994
Hank Aaron
Sparky Anderson
Harley Bowers
Jimmy Bragan
Lou Brissie
Steve Carlton
Ty Cobb
Julian Fine
Danny Hayling
Harmon Killebrew
Don Mattingly
John Moss
Spec Richardson
Frank Robinson
Nolan Ryan
Ryne Sandberg
Willie Stargell

Class of 1995
Bob Bonifay
Dave Bristol
Cecil Darby
Bob Gibson
Goose Goslin
Al Lopez
Enos Slaughter
Don Stafford

Class of 1996
Jim Bayens
Bill Bethea
Ed Holtz
Roy Majtyka
Pat Putnam
Hoyt Wilhelm
Pat Williams

CLASS OF 1997
Red Dwyer
Billy Johnson
Dale Murphy

CLASS OF 1998
Sheldon Bender
Dwight Lowry
Charles Morrow
Michael Paterno
Mel Roberts
Gene Sapakoff
Marty Springstead

CLASS OF 1999
Ron McKee
Eddie Murray
Paul Snyder

CLASS OF 2000
Doc Kanupp
Pat O'Conner
Mike Szemplenski
Bob Terrell

CLASS OF 2001
Smokey Alston
Wilt Browning
Murray Cook
Gordo Gordon
Charlie Harville
Tommy Lasorda

CLASS OF 2002
Bill Blackwell
Winston Blenckstone
Larry Bowa
Dan O'Brien
Joe West

CLASS OF 2003
Don Beaver
Happy Chandler
Doug Flynn
Ken Kaiser
Phil Niekro
Branch Rickey

CLASS OF 2004
Dick Butler
Marvin Goldklang
Elaine Moss
Earl Williams

CLASS OF 2005
Bobby Bonds
Drew Coble
Jack Farnsworth
Bob Hager
Marcus Holland
Alan Stein

CLASS OF 2006
Len Barker
Chip Moore
Aaron Pointer
Mike Veeck

CLASS OF 2007
Chipper Jones
Jack Hiatt
Leo Hughes
R. E. Littlejohn
Scoop Oliver
Verner Ross

CLASS OF 2008
Buddy Bell
Vince Coleman
Bing Devine
Johnnie Shives
Matthew Winters

National Baseball Hall of Fame Members from the SAL

What would baseball be without the National Baseball Hall of Fame in Cooperstown? Where else could you see the baseball that Ruth hit a mile and a half with a fungo? Or the bicycle that Harvey Wallbanger rode back and forth between home and the ballpark while playing his way to the Hall of Fame? (That, of course, was before anyone ever dreamed of million-dollar salaries.) Many of the baseball greats enshrined in the National Baseball Hall of Fame in Cooperstown got their start in professional baseball in the South Atlantic League. They are listed here alphabetically.

Hank Aaron
Sparky Anderson
Steve Carlton
Happy Chandler
Ty Cobb
Bob Gibson
Goose Goslin
Harmon Killebrew
Tommy Lasorda
Al Lopez
Eddie Murray
Phil Niekro
Branch Rickey
Frank Robinson
Nolan Ryan
Ryne Sandberg
Enos Slaughter
Willie Stargell
Hoyt Wilhelm

ABOUT THE AUTHOR

A native of Sylva, North Carolina, Bob Terrell has lived all his life in Western North Carolina. After attending Western Carolina University, he joined the staff of *The Asheville Citizen-Times* as a sports reporter in 1949 and spent thirty-seven years full time for that newspaper. He spent twenty years as sports editor and baseball writer, covering the Asheville Tourists and other teams in the South Atlantic, Tri-State, Southern, and Western Carolina leagues. Bob was inducted into the South Atlantic League Hall of Fame as a baseball writer in 2000.

It has been estimated that Terrell has written more than eighteen million words in the newspaper. When Bob retired from writing daily columns, he started writing books and has produced over seventy in the last thirty years. His works include biographies, westerns, and collections of his newspaper columns–columns which often related the humorous incidents of everyday life.

Another favorite pastime of Bob's is traveling, especially to Israel and the Mideast. Bob lives in Asheville and has three grown sons.